MOTHER, MADONNA, WHORE

Motherhood confers unequalled powers which some women misuse because of their own emotional problems and the social expectations placed upon them. Some mothers batter their children; others commit incest with them. Physical abuse is only one of the ways mothers damage their children. Another is to prevent them from understanding or accepting their core gender-identity.

Estela Welldon believes that mothers often see their children as extensions of themselves, and that mothers' mistreatment of their children is a form of self-inflicted wound. The children's problems are traced to the problems of the mother and these, in turn, are traced to the problems she had with her own mother.

Provocative and disturbing, *Mother, Madonna, Whore* poses new questions about the nature and origins of female perversion. Drawing on many years' experience at one of the world's leading therapeutic centres for work with sexual and social deviants, Dr Welldon explains the dynamics of how some girls become perverse women; and how they view their relations with their own bodies, their parents, children and lovers. At the deepest level she touches on the complex issue of the origins of child abuse, incest and prostitution.

The table of contents includes: Female Sexual Perversion; Sexuality and the Female Body; The Power of the Womb; Motherhood as a Perversion; Mothers who Commit Incest; The Symbolic Mother as Whore; Substitute Motherhood.

Estela V. Welldon is a Fellow of the Royal College of Psychiatrists and Consultant Psychotherapist and Clinical Tutor at the Portman Clinic, London, a National Health Service centre specializing in the dynamic psychotherapy of sexual deviance and criminality. She is also in private practice and runs women's groups on the Continent.

MOTHER, MADONNA, WHORE

The Idealization and
Denigration of
Motherhood

Estela V. Welldon

'an association in which the free development of each
is the condition for the free development of all'

Free Association Books / London / 1988

First published in Great Britain 1988 by
Free Association Books
26 Freegrove Road
London N7 9RQ

© Estela V. Welldon 1988

British Library Cataloguing in Publication Data

Welldon, Estela V.
  Mother, madonna, whore: the idealization
  and denigration of motherhood
  1. Motherhood. Psychological aspects
  I. Title
  155.6'463

ISBN 1-85343-039-0
ISBN 1-85343-040-4 Pbk

Typeset by AKM Associates (UK) Ltd,
Ajmal House, Hayes Road, Southall, London.
Printed and bound in Great Britain by
Short Run Press Ltd, Exeter

Much is owed to friends and colleagues, but it does not compare with the debt I owe my patients. It is to them that I dedicate this book, in gratitude, and also in the hope that it will help others who are suffering or might come to suffer from the painful predicaments of my patients.

CONTENTS

ACKNOWLEDGEMENTS

Every author constitutes a one-parent family, and, of course, I have sole responsibility for my child. But this particular child has had many aunts, uncles and grandparents. Some have taken great pains to help; others have assisted unknowingly. Some have contributed to the gestation of the project; others have encouraged its development; and still others have given it a degree of coherence and polish which I could not have achieved on my own. Some, indeed, have influenced the project at every stage of its many-layered development: I have been greatly sustained by Dr Earl Hopper, whose confidence and important insights have been crucial; Gregorio Kohon has also been a perceptive and constructive commentator throughout.

If this book can be said to have had a beginning, it sprang from the decision in 1978 of the Chairman of the Portman Clinic, Dr Mervin Glasser, to make me responsible for the first seminars at the Clinic on female perversions. My experience at the Portman of diagnosing and treating problems relating to perversions and criminality showed me how many more male than female patients there were, and this helped to set me thinking. The resulting ideas formed the subject of numerous discussions with my colleagues at the Portman Clinic, and I am grateful to them all for their illuminating comments. These ideas expanded and took form in a lecture on 'motherhood and sexual perversion', which many of my colleagues — amongst them Luisa Alvarez de Toledo, Pamela Ashurst, Fern Cramer-Azima, Maria Dufau-Catt, Florencio Escardo, Zaida Hall, Louise Kaplan, Moises Lemlij, Adam Limentani, Terry Lear, Norman Morris, Marisa Pastorino, Jonathan Pedder, Malcolm Pines, Bart de Smit, Frank Tait, Patrick Woodcock, and Monica Zureti — read with discernment. I would especially like to thank Dr Janine Puget for her comments and support. An invitation in 1985 to deliver the same lecture at The Menninger Foundation at Topeka, Kansas, where I had received much of my formative training, took my understanding a stage further. I am particularly grateful to Drs Ramon Ganzarain, Bonnie Buchele, and Larry Kennedy for their generous comments and for putting me in touch with much recent relevant literature.

I must acknowledge an influence of a different sort, but no less potent. I have several women friends who have nothing to do with this profession, but who nevertheless have had a major influence on whether or not I persisted, in the midst of distractions, self-induced and otherwise, with so ambitious a project. They, in particular, Helena Kennedy and Georgia Brown, have made me feel in a vivid way that they are interested in my conclusions, and I am grateful to them all whether this was their intention or not.

In the final stages of this curious process of turning thoughts and experiences into a well-baked cake with precisely defined slices or chapters, a special contribution was made by Sally Belfrage, who knows how to put together a book and what it is to be feminine in the modern world.

Facts must — and, I hope, do — underline presentation, style, and argument. Margaret Walker and her team of the Tavistock Clinic library have given generously of their time, and I have benefited from their enormous experience, good humour, and lasting patience. Over the years others have helped my accuracy, like the clerical staff at the Portman, notably Judy Wilkins. Many of them knew what I was aiming for almost before I did.

There may be some, eminent or otherwise, who have not
been adequately acknowledged in this note. I beg their pardons
and can only say that the material in this book belongs to many
people.

I HAVE FOUND MYSELF recalling a remark made to me a long time ago by a man given to reflections on the oddities of the human race. He thought it remarkable that, even though the two sexes had looked at each other throughout all recorded time, they still seemed unable to understand each other. I wonder if this sour half-truth is not partly justified by the tendency of each sex to project on to the other its expectations of its own kind? In a world where it has been the prerogative of men to teach and to write books, this would partly account for the continued poverty of our understanding about the predicaments of women. It is not that women have been neglected, rather that false assumptions have been made and women as well as men have been ready to accept them. However, these assumptions may have different origins.

Psychoanalysis gave us access to the unconscious mind and to the motivations underlying our actions. Then we optimistically believed that we had been enriched in our understanding of the opposite sex and were nearer to a mutual self-knowledge. This proved to be a premature assumption; the search for this enlightenment is still in a developmental stage.

Freud — the originator of all these invaluable discoveries — though a genius, was as a man unable to convey a full understanding of the complexities in the libidinal developments of the two genders. He made the Oedipus complex, based on the male model, the bedrock of normal libidinal development. According to Freud, this complex occurs in the phallic stage, between the ages of three and five. It is based on a dual desire: firstly for the parent of the opposite sex, and secondly for the death of the parent of the same sex, which will then enable the boy to possess his mother. The child fears the father's retaliation for these murderous wishes; castration seems the unavoidable outcome. The only satisfactory way to resolve castration anxieties is to renounce the incestuous object, so the Oedipus complex comes to an end and the boy enters the latency period. This is a traditional theory which is still used by many practitioners, not only in relation to normal sexuality but also in the understanding of its perverse manifestations.

This theory has two main foci: firstly the phallus as *the* genital organ, and secondly the position of the child in a triangular relationship in which he first tries to conquer his mother, but eventually has to accept a position outside the parental unit. It was first applied to the boy's libidinal development, but was soon transplanted to the girl's. A 'parallel' situation to that in boys was created in girls with the inception of 'penis-envy'. The girl enters into the Oedipus complex directed by the castration complex. She changes not only her sexual object from mother to father, but also her wish for the penis her mother never gave her for a wish to have a baby by her father. *The symbolic equivalence of penis and baby was created.*

Freud himself thought that female sexuality was a 'riddle'. He asked his women colleagues to enlighten him about their own sexuality since he thought they had the advantage of being suitable 'mother-substitutes' during the transference process with their patients. This was in itself an odd request since, as Schafer has noted, '. . . He [Freud] continued to neglect the essentially androgynous role of the psychoanalyst in the transference . . . There is little evidence of Freud's having been alert to or impressed by maternal transference to the male

MOTHER,
MADONNA,
WHORE

analyst — or, for that matter, by maternal counter-transference
on the part of the male analyst' (1974, p. 477). And later:

Freud was not prepared to think about mothers very far ... he showed virtually no sustained interest in their subjective experience – except for their negative feelings about their own femininity and worth and their compensatory cravings to be loved and impregnated, especially with sons ... It seems that he knew the father and the castrate in himself and other men but not the mother and the woman. (p. 482)

The response of Freud's female colleagues was overwhelming. Many women psychoanalysts were stimulated to come forward with new ideas full of originality and richness, some agreeing and others disagreeing with Freud's postulations. It was most unfortunate, though, that these were not heard as voices of legitimate female self-assertion, but instead were taken as voices of dissent. Among the first to speak out was Horney who, in her paper 'On the genesis of castration complex in women', says '. . . an assertion that one half of the human race is discontented with the sex assigned to it and can overcome this discontent only in favourable circumstances — is decidedly unsatisfying, not only to feminine narcissisms but also to biological science' (1924, p. 38).

Many papers and books have recently been published showing that women psychoanalysts made important contributions, Riviere (1929), Brierley (1932, 1936), and Payne (1935) among them. At the same time Deutsch (1925, 1930) and Lampl de Groot (1928, 1933), and later Brunswick (1940) — all women psychoanalysts, acknowledged the influence of the pre-oedipal mother and noted Freud's failure to pay sufficient attention to the obvious effect the archaic, powerful, controlling mother has on the child (see Barglow and Schaefer, 1970).

For their part, Horney (1924, 1926, 1932, 1933), Muller (1932), and Barnett (1966), rather than simply seeing the little girl as lacking a penis, wrote about her experiencing vaginal sensations and impulses that made her feel feminine from the beginning. From her own clinical experiences with adult

4 women, Greenacre (1950) developed the view that vaginal awareness is present in females well before puberty.

These professional women offered important insights about the functioning female body and its symbolic operation in a woman's inner world. Together they can be said to have established an alternative theoretical system. But it was to no avail. The psychoanalytical world of ideas by then belonged to men — the supremacy of the phallus had won unlimited, unquestionable, and irrefutable acceptance. Traditional psychoanalysis seemed not to be influenced by what these women had to say, although their ideas about their own territory were so much more sophisticated and innovative than what men had previously said. Within the psychoanalytical movement these ideas appeared in obscure papers which attracted little attention. Indeed, women psychoanalysts were relegated to practice in their field as 'mother-substitutes' and caretakers of patients; they were not supposed to postulate new theories. Whereas the penis is considered as an anatomical reality, the term 'phallus' is used as an embracing symbol meaning all power; such was the dominance of men in the world of ideas and philosophy, it became natural to accept the superior power of the phallus. The women's theories have been revived only in the past two decades, mostly as a result of pressures from the women's movement rather than from the world of psychoanalysis. Before then women had to listen to and acquiesce in the theories of the male masters. Other workers in this field still refer to the disagreements over female sexuality between Freud (1905, 1931, 1933) and Jones (1927), but their female contemporaries' ideas are treated with ignorance or patronizing indifference.

The relative positions of the two sexes in society are very different, as clearly indicated by Erikson: 'Woman, through the ages (at any rate, the patriarchal ones), has lent herself to a variety of roles conducive to an exploitation of masochistic potentials: she has let herself be confined and immobilized, enslaved and infantilized, prostituted and exploited, deriving from it at best what in psychopathology we call "secondary gains" of devious dominance' (1968, p. 284). Or, as Schafer puts it, '. . . human sexuality is indeed *psychosexuality* . . .

Psychosexuality means mental sexuality, that is, a sexuality of
meanings and personal relationships that have developed and
been organized around real and imagined experiences and
situations in a social world . . . This centring on ultimate
procreative genitality explains some of the imperfections of
Freud's psychology of women . . .' (1974, pp. 472–3, author's
italics).

It is only within the past fifteen years that important
theories about female sexuality and perversions postulated by
female colleagues such as Chasseguet-Smirgel (1985a, 1985b)
and McDougall (1986) have been published and taken seriously by our profession. They have had an enormous and
welcome influence on both ideas and practice.

Within the traditional psychoanalytical framework — that
is, Freud's theories — perversion in males is viewed as the result
of an unresolved Oedipus complex which has castration
anxiety as its central and main component. When the oedipal
male reaches manhood, he is unable to reach genital primacy
with a person of the opposite sex, since his mother is still in his
unconscious mind, and he feels in extreme anxiety of being
castrated by his father. He then denies the differentiation of the
sexes and creates a phallic mother.

The traditional theory with its 'imposed parallelism'
between boys and girls was abandoned by other investigators in
the light of the systematic studies of observations of the
mother–baby unit and the awareness of the importance for
both sexes of the period of attachment to the mother, the
so-called 'pre-oedipal' phase. This phase is currently thought
to account for perverse psychopathology of males, in which the
psychogenesis is deeply related to intense fears of being either
abandoned or seduced by the mother. There is still no
acknowledgement of female perversion, though the evidence is
that male perversion is often the result of early faulty mothering. Why is it so difficult to conceptualize the notion of perverse
motherhood and other female perverse behaviour according to
a separate, completely different psychopathology which origin-
ates from the female body and its inherent attributes? Male
assumptions have made it difficult to understand some female
behaviour, including female perversions, sometimes to the

6   extent of denying all evidence that female perversions exist. Perhaps the reason why the female experiences identified in the chapters that follow have only rarely been diagnosed is that there is a long tradition of seeing women's sexual development as parallel to men's — whatever was considered normal for men was supposed to be so for women.

This book is a study of the neglected area of female perversions, based on twenty years of clinical work with women patients. Before we come to the detailed argument, it is important to recognize that there is a difference between the everyday and psychoanalytical uses of the term 'perversion'. Whereas ordinarily the word is supposed to be pejorative and carries moral implications, in psychoanalysis it means simply a dysfunction of the sexual component of personality development. (In contrast, 'deviation', a term often used interchangeably with 'perversion', implies a statistical abnormality; it describes an act not *usually* performed in certain circumstances within a given cultural milieu. I must stress that I use 'perversion' in the psychoanalytical sense. This is very different from a classical neurotic or psychotic condition, which is why I shall insist on using the term 'perversion', for it defines the existence of some specific and characteristic features. However, Storr, among other authorities, prefers to use the term 'deviation' when referring to perversion. He says: 'It is the compulsive substitution of something else for heterosexual intercourse in circumstances where the latter is available which chiefly characterizes the behaviour we call sexually *deviant*' (1964, p. 13, my italics).

Perversion is 'any form of adult sexual behaviour in which heterosexual is not the preferred goal', as simply described by Rycroft (1968, p. 116). The definition of perversion varies slightly from author to author. For I. Rosen (1979a, p. 32) it should always include the final pathway of sexual discharge leading to genital orgasm, whereas Laplanche and Pontalis have a more comprehensive view: they see perversion as encompassing 'the whole of psychosexual behaviour that accompanies such atypical means of obtaining sexual pleasure' (1973, p. 306). The former descriptions fit men. However, they become almost impossible to apply to women since they sometimes use the function of 'heterosexual intercourse' for perverse aims. It is well known that the definition of 'true sexual perversion' should always include the participation of the body. In other words, fantasies about bizarre or perverse actions are not enough to be labelled as perverse. The 'body barrier' means that the individual must use the body for the perverse action. However, I believe that the term 'body' in the definition of perversion has been mistakenly identified exclusively with the male anatomy and physiology, specifically with the penis and genital orgasm. How could we otherwise have overlooked the fact that women's bodies are completely taken over in the course of their inherent functioning by procreative drives, sometimes accompanied with the most perverse fantasies, whose outcome materializes in their bodies?

Since men had appealed to perversion as a way to deal with the fears of losing their penis, women were left in a position in which perversions were not available to them. As women do not have a penis, so the argument went, they must have a different type of Oedipus complex and castration anxiety. Hence the then popular view that 'Women can't have sexual perversions since they don't possess a penis' was seldom questioned. Freud theorized that the Oedipus complex was resolved in little girls when they fantasized having Daddy's babies inside themselves. Developing his ideas, we could say provocatively that 'Women can't have perversions because they can have babies.'

In trying to describe perversion, I shall place the main emphasis on understanding the perverse individual. We shall look at some landmarks in psychological development, and I shall speculate on how these link with the form and content of the perverse action. At the same time we shall have to bear in mind that, in both sexes, perversion involves a deep split between genital sexuality as a living — or loving — force and what appears to be sexual, but actually corresponds to much more primitive stages where pregenitality pervades the whole picture.

In male perversion this profound split is between what the individual experiences as his anatomical maturity, and his mental representations of his body in which he sees himself as a

8 raging and desperate baby. Hence, although he responds physically with a genital orgasm, the fantasies in his mind belong to pre-oedipal stages.

Later on in life, when he appears very much an adult, he is ready for revenge. He is not consciously aware of this hatred. Indeed, usually he does not understand what 'is taking him over' or why he does 'those things' which actually provide him with no pleasure beyond a short-lived feeling of well-being, though that lasts long enough for him to experience a sense of relief from his mounting anxiety. He does not know why a particular, sometimes bizarre activity, which he knows is wrong, makes him feel better. It is all the more puzzling to him when there are so many alternatives which would obviously be more satisfactory and more socially acceptable. He is only too painfully aware of the compulsion to repeat the action, but he is quite oblivious of the hostility that causes it. Furthermore, knowledge of whom he hates and on whom he wants to take revenge remains deep in his unconscious.

So far what I have said refers to both sexes, but I shall have to introduce some modifications in order to illustrate what goes on in the female world. Accurate diagnosis of these conditions in women has hitherto been lacking; it was as if we were afraid of reaching a deeper understanding — perhaps because, as I have suggested, women were seen as being incapable of committing perversions.

As a clinician I have observed that the main difference between a male and female perverse action lies in the aim. Whereas in men the act is aimed at an outside part-object, in women it is usually against themselves, either against their bodies or against objects which they see as their own creations: their babies. In both cases, bodies and babies are treated as part-objects.

For the purpose of authenticity and emphasis, I shall use the 'uncustomary' pronoun 'she' when referring to patterns of feeling or behaviour that apply equally to both sexes.

The perverse person feels that she has not been allowed to enjoy a sense of her own development as a separate individual, with her own identity; in other words she has not experienced the freedom to be herself. This creates in her the deep belief that

she is not a whole being, but her mother's part-object, just as
she experienced her mother when she was a very young infant.
From early on in her life she felt unwanted, undesired, and
ignored, or alternatively a very important but almost unidenti-
fiable part of her parents' lives (usually her mother's). In this
last case she will feel smothered and 'overprotected' (which
actually means totally unprotected). Both situations create
enormous insecurity and vulnerability, and induce an intense
hatred of the person who inflicted them on her, and who was
the most important being when she was a baby — her mother.

From being victims, such people become the victimizers. In
their actions they are the perpetrators of the victimization and
humiliation previously inflicted on them. They treat their
victims in the same way they felt treated themselves: as part-
objects who are there only to satisfy their whims and bizarre
expectations. Such apparent sexual acting-out is a manic
defence against formidable fears related to the threat of losing
both mother and a sense of identity.

The main feature of perversion is that, symbolically, the
individual through her perverse action tries to conquer a
tremendous fear of losing her mother. As a baby she never felt
safe with her mother, but instead at her most vulnerable,
experiencing her mother as a very dangerous person. Consequently the underlying motivation in perversion is a hostile,
sadistic one. This unconscious mechanism is characteristic of
the perverse mind.

My argument is drawn entirely from my own clinical
experience. But now that it has led me to some understanding
of female perversion and the causes of it, not least in
inadequate mothering, it is evident to me that some of the
difficulties that have so far prevented the evidence from being
accepted for what it is arose from a particular and social
milieu. It is not my intention to write social history, but it is
hard to avoid the conclusions that in our time we have
witnessed grave inconsistencies in the way we view women,
their emotional needs, and their biological–reproductive
functions.

For example, I remember all too clearly the 1960s and the
way Laing's (1961) theory about 'schizophrenogenic' mothers

10   was misinterpreted and used by both professional and lay persons to blame such women. The theory claimed that these mothers were sending contradictory messages (which Bateson (1956) had earlier termed 'double bind') to their babies. Consequently, confusion prevailed in those babies' minds; they felt their mothers never allowed them to know what was right or wrong. A psychotic organization of their minds was beginning. At the time, both professional and lay opinion was that an 'understanding' of these schizophrenic patients had now become easily available, so much so that they became 'the prophets of a new world'. But what about their mothers? They were automatically considered responsible for their children's condition. They got no real or compassionate understanding; they were to be 'condemned' for their 'bad' behaviour. But only a few outside the clinical profession remembered that these mothers had been through traumatic experiences earlier in their own lives, which had partly led to 'double bind' attitudes towards their children. They had been victims and in turn were producing more victims.

Again in the 1960s, we neglected to acknowledge what really happened with 'battered babies'; nobody, even experienced physicians, could believe that those babies' injuries had been caused by their mothers. No one seemed to understand these women as mothers: 'women' were seen as capable of such actions, but not 'mothers'. But of course they were daughters and women first, some of whom just by sheer chance had become mothers. The failure accurately to diagnose such women came, I believe, partly from society's glorification of motherhood, its refusal to admit that motherhood could have any negative aspects.

Two decades on, we are similarly failing to admit the possibility of maternal incest. Everyone is ready to recognize paternal incest, which as far as we know is much more common, but not what mothers do. Nobody believes it is happening — sometimes even to the mother's chagrin.

To understand the problems of perversion and motherhood which are the central themes of this book, we have to free ourselves from some of the assumptions — both professional and social — that I have mentioned, and return to basics. We

must begin with the female body and its inherent attributes. It
will not then seem strange to discover that women have a completely different psychopathology from men.

In my examination of women's psychopathology I shall focus on this more primitive level of libidinal development. The perverse individual has been prevented, from a very early age, from achieving sexual emotional maturity (that is, genital sexuality) and consequently has difficulties in forming satisfactory heterosexual relationships. This fact is crucial in the understanding of perversion. I have observed, during the course of therapy and from the type of transference which emerges in this particular group of patients, how fundamental is that very early relationship with the mother. At this stage the father takes a secondary role. As I shall explain, this changes later on, especially in adolescence.

I shall follow the object-relations theory, put forward by Klein and others, which stresses the importance of the first few months of life and the infant–mother relationship, and how the defence mechanisms the baby uses at that time persist throughout life and are crucial to emotional and libidinal development.

Regarding female sexuality, I adhere to the ideas of Jones (1927), M. Klein (1928, 1932, 1933, 1935), Horney (1924, 1926, 1932, 1933) and others, who not only question the primacy of penis-envy in the little girl but also stress her early unconscious awareness of her vagina. Klein links this with an extremely early oedipal development. Her theories centre on the infant girl's intense envy of her mother's reproductive functions. This creates in her a great hostility directed towards her mother, and develops into frustrated fantasies of entering her mother's body and robbing it of its entire contents. Using projective mechanisms, she assumes that her mother will rob her of her own procreative capacities. I have observed the occurrence of those mental mechanisms in the women I treat, and believe they become the equivalent of castration fears in the boy.

Baby girls as well as baby boys can be subjected to situations which may lead them, in adult life, into perverse attitudes or perversions. But women have the opportunity, when they

12 become mothers, to perform perverting actions towards their babies.

It is with these general considerations in mind that the structure of the following chapters has been determined. Chapter 2 concentrates on the idea that the quality of their bodies and of their offspring is fundamental to women's psychology; it is crucial that the female body is specially designed to produce and nurture babies. The chapter also stresses that women's reproductive organs are more widely located than men's. M. Pines puts it thus:

Contrasting the little boy's and the little girl's bodies, Deutsch stresses the manner in which the penis is discovered early, is constantly stimulated, and becomes an erotogenic zone before it is ready to fulfil its biological functions . . . Because the clitoris is an unsatisfactory sexual organ, it cannot arrogate to itself as much libido as the penis. Owing to this 'lesser tyranny' of the clitoris, a female through her life may remain more infantile, and for her the whole body may remain a sexual organ. (1969, p. 5, my emphasis)

These are old-fashioned ideas which stress the importance of penis-envy and the sense of inferiority that women experience in their sexual development, but, even so, the whole female body is acknowledged as a sexual organ.

We know that women frequently act as if their whole body were a sexual organ. Pathological cases include a wide range of attacks by women on their own bodies which can be seen as perverse: for example anorexia, bulimia, and self-mutilation. It is well known that these conditions occur more often in women than in men. They are accompanied by disturbances of the menses, which can be indicators of unresolved problems these women have, not only about their body images but also about accepting their sexuality and its inherent biological functions.

Chapter 3 takes the argument a stage further by stressing the power of the womb. It has no less power than the phallus, but operates in a different way. The mother–baby unit is at a biological–psychological peak when the mother is ready with

her breasts filled with milk just as her baby is being awakened
by hunger. Both parties get together, and a world of bliss is open to them. Of course, having accepted the reality principle we know that the two individuals will never be able to relive these moments in quite the same way. We may try to reproduce this Utopian situation, but the older we become the more we grow to appreciate that our expectations are necessarily limited. However, some people have not come to accept the reality principle because as babies they went through too many frustrating and damaging experiences; even now they are still seeking a promised land of bliss, but treading many dangerous paths in their quest. This is the first layer of what takes place in the fantasy world of the perverse. But the whole situation is more complicated, as we realize when we encounter the overriding element of sadistic revenge, so poignantly described by Stoller (1975) as 'the erotic form of hatred'.

This leads to Chapter 4 on motherhood and sexual perversion, which might be considered the heart of the book. As such, it should speak for itself.

The later chapters deal with the causes and consequences of the condition described in Chapter 4. They consider both maternal and paternal incest (Chapter 5) with its frequent consequence, prostitution (Chapter 7). They also discuss the problems of the men who frequent prostitutes and the relationship between client and prostitute (Chapter 6). These are difficult questions which have until recently been largely submerged under social taboos, but they are clearly related to the central theme. My findings in this area are, like the rest of the book, the result of clinical experience and my reflections on it.

If this hypothesis has something to contribute to the professional understanding of the predicament of some women, it is entirely because of the evidence presented by those women who for one reason or another have become my patients. Some may think that the clinical vignettes offered here are exceptional or extreme examples of women in distress. Indeed, some of them are, but the quality of their tribulations is shared to some degree by many other women who do not dare to talk openly in front of men about such difficulties. They prefer to keep their inner thoughts to themselves rather than risk rejection and misunderstanding. My aim is that the predicaments in which some women have found themselves, and for which they themselves have been blamed, should be more widely recognized. It is not my intention to write about their treatment. That is another subject, and one which merits separate consideration in the future. But I do hope that, in the meanwhile, some of my comments will suggest a different diagnostic approach.

The writing of this book about female sexual perversion has become for me a matter of great professional concern, as in my clinical practice I have come to learn more and more about women, their needs, and aspects of their sexuality. Women come to me with emotional difficulties which, though not always immediately related to sexuality, are often found to be linked to it when their problems are studied in depth. For, despite the vast increase in the understanding of women brought about by the world's many feminist movements, most women still find it very difficult to talk about sexually related problems for fear of being misunderstood. This fear partly reflects their own confusion and shame, and partly the still considerable lack of knowledge on the subject.

I shall write only about the problems of women I know. They are related, not only directly to their sexuality, but also to their frustration, insecurity, and loneliness. Sometimes my patients have covered up these bitter conflicts so well that for a long time they have not been able to obtain support, let alone professional help. At other times they have tried to win a vicarious sense of power through a variety of actions which left them with only a feeling of great shame.

The women I treat come from all walks of life. Some are referred for problems specifically related to sexuality. Others spontaneously seek professional help with conflicts to do with their lives in general, and still others come because of difficulties in their personal relationships. Referral agencies send patients because of problems related to the law. Some women politely refuse to admit to needing any help; this is usually a sign of their own low self-esteem and leads them to maintain that they should not be taken too seriously. However they have come to me, many of these women have been in intensive psychotherapy for some time, and in the course of psychotherapy the problems which I shall try to describe begin to emerge.

Most of the women I see are not obviously psychotic, nor do they suffer from complete ego disintegration. They could be considered to be borderline–narcissistic personalities of various degrees of severity. Some have been able to pursue professional careers, and also to achieve relationships, though they themselves consider these unsatisfactory; others have been able to lead only a precarious existence in the outside world.

My experience in learning about women has been enriched by interacting as a group analyst with certain groups of professional women on the Continent who are in much less need of help than most of my patients in London. The object of the participants is to get to know themselves better and thus to achieve happier lives. In addition, they want to feel what it is to be in an all-women's group. This has been a courageous and, I think, successful enterprise. The degree of intimacy and trust which prevails in these groups is exceptional. The way these women express their feelings and voice their difficulties, either by identifying with or in confrontation with other women, is markedly different from the way they communicate when they are in mixed company. The group sometimes provides a way of containing secrets, traumas, shame, disappointment. At other times it gives the women the freedom to talk about their successes, achievements and sense of contentment in their domestic or professional lives, despite the fear of provoking the envy of the other women, a reminder of their own mothers' envy.

This book is partly a result of my finding through these groups that the difficulties which 'women with severe problems' bring to me in my clinical practice are shared to some degree by many other women. There is often a failure to consider the special problems women face in getting to know themselves — problems exacerbated by the various and multiple demands made on them in their important role of being intimate, not only as women but also as mothers. To acquire self-knowledge of their own womanhood in a way that is separate from their motherhood seems to many women a luxury that is impossible to achieve, perhaps because both their minds and their bodies are so much more involved than would be the case for men.

Experience with these groups of women has brought home to me that not everything is to be explained solely in terms of biological or psychological factors. Social structures and cultural environments also play a part. Indeed, I make a plea, following Hopper (1986), for the consistent application of the sociological insight that an intrapsychic phenomenon must be viewed on an appropriately long timescale and with full account taken of socio-psychological aspects. At least a three-generational approach is required, and it should include also the variety of social and cultural phenomena that confer importance on motherhood as the main source of power and control available to women. In my field, it is impossible to gain a complete understanding of psychopathological behaviour originating in the mother–baby unit without a knowledge of events in the mother's and maternal grandmother's early lives.

The function of motherhood has given some women the opportunity to exercise 'perverting' attitudes towards their babies, using them as extensions of their own bodies for unconscious needs of their own. These phenomena are the result of combined psychological, physiological, biological, social, historical, and cultural factors. But considerations of the same general kind have prevented us from fully acknow-ledging female perverse behaviour. We have all become silent conspirators in a system in which change could not be envisaged since no one would acknowledge that such behaviour existed. This failure has deprived some women of a better understanding of their difficulties.

I offer my findings cautiously. I did not start out to investigate, still less to establish a theory. I simply took note of the evidence that came before me in clinical practice. I found this evidence surprising in the light of the existing theories about perversion, especially in relation to women, and began to feel a need to record and order my observations and then to make sense of them. The present book is the result. Despite my commitment to my personal observations, I know that I am by no means the only practitioner in the field, and I hope my comments reflect this recognition. I am also aware that my clinical material and observations are sometimes controversial, and that consequently, for one reason or another, my observations may meet with misunderstanding and disapproval. This is painful but probably inevitable with this particular type of psychopathology, which has only just begun to be studied. Nevertheless, I should like to avoid unnecessary controversy as much as I can. Even so, since my main responsibility remains to my patients, I must honour what they have taught me and try to teach others how to recognize, if necessary to avoid, the kinds of problems which they have had the courage to reveal to me.

This other side of motherhood, or 'perverse mothering', will be examined not only as it occurs in real life, but also in some of its many symbolic representations. The re-enacting in adulthood of some of the aspects of the mother–infant relationship can lead to grotesque manifestations in which the early relationship is caricatured. Such is the case with some forms of female prostitution. This will emerge in Chapter 6 as another neglected problem, one which concerns not only the prostitutes but also the men who pursue them. The problems for both are traceable to a common root — early faulty mothering, which could be the result of a family background of emotional deprivation and a threat to gender recognition. Sometimes incest provides a type of substitute 'mothering' experience as described in Chapter 7. Some girls who have had this experience see prostitution as the only survival mechanism. Whatever these women's backgrounds, a splitting process is in full operation, together with a feeling of elation at being in complete control and in a dominant position in which revenge, conscious or unconscious, is the driving force. These are manic defences used to counteract a hidden mourning process associated with feelings of helplessness and hopelessness that these girls encountered when they were very young and abused, and which were then repressed.

We should not be surprised at the existence of this 'other side' of motherhood. Women are expected to carry out the difficult and responsible task of motherhood without having

18 had much, if any, emotional preparation for it. Their responsibility is to bring up healthy and stable babies who will adapt happily and adequately to growing external demands. In fact women really are in too lonely a position to deliver the goods properly, and this marks a fundamental difference between men and women. After all, it is within the first few months of the relationship with its mother that the growing infant will acquire the psychological rudiments on which its adult relationships will be based. But this process will take place whether or not the mother is herself stable and emotionally mature. Irrespective of the mother's upbringing, it is always assumed that 'maternal instinct' will come to the fore and will perform miracles. Or, in Kestenberg's words, '. . . our ideal picture of a truly maternal woman is one of an omnipotent, all-knowing mother who knows what to do with her infant by sheer intuition' (1956, p. 260).

Mothers are expected by society to behave as if they had been provided with magic wands which not only free them from previous conflicts, but also equip them to deal with the new emergencies of motherhood with skill, precision, and dexterity. Why is it so difficult for us to see that, for some women, motherhood intensifies their previous problems to the point where they are unable to cope any more? They know nothing about babies, except that with their arrival they are supposed to find fulfilment and happiness, even if there is also some distress and practical inconvenience. Fulfilment and happiness often are achieved, but sometimes unconsciously an old, painful experience resurfaces. A terrible sense of despair, despondency, and inadequacy can easily turn into hatred and revenge directed at the new baby.

The more I have listened to women fumbling, usually in the dark, with their special problems, the more convinced I have become that as a caring society we need to bridge the large gap that exists between what we already know of female sexuality and the full truth about women and the vicissitudes of their sexual experience.

SEXUALITY AND THE FEMALE BODY

THE ORGANS used for reproduction also trigger off the dynamics of sexual gratification. Many individuals take that for granted. However, some people cannot integrate into their mental representations of their bodies either the real or the symbolic connection between the discharge of sexual tension and its effects on their reproductive organs. Moreover, some are quite oblivious to any correlation between the two. They have failed to perceive how their inner lives could be enriched in the interaction with the outside world through their sexual organs by intimacy with a person of the opposite sex.

Orgasm is an invaluable means for couples to come together, emotionally and physically. Not only does it create an incomparable physical closeness in which mutual trust prevails, but also the differentiation of the sexes is truly acknowledged and accepted as complementary.

> So love has made us one
> And being one has made us whole.

In such a relationship there is also a myriad of inner events which reveal many fantasies and wonders about the intricacies and mysteries of the Other. When it works, this produces an incredible wealth for both parties.

Knowledge of this realm is essential for the early development of gender-identity. For some people this is obvious. Eventually, as the relationship grows emotionally, they have in mind not only their bodies but also the reproductive functions attached to them. It is then that they start to fantasize about the creation of a new human being who will possess emotional and physical characteristics representing both of them and who, they hope, will bring them still closer together. Bibring *et al.* drew attention to the fact that 'an intense object-relationship to the sexual partner leads to the event of impregnation, by which a significant representation of the love-object becomes part of the self' (1961, p. 15).

But many other people do not share this wish/hope/dream. They put their bodies at the service of fast gratification of their sexual needs in an explosive and impulsive way, without attending to the loving aspects. Notwithstanding the use of reproductive organs in those actions, the male perverse individual does not profit from positive mental symbolic representations of his reproductive organs; this extra dimension is simply not available to him.

For a woman, though, it is quite a different matter. She knows from the very primitive roots of her feminine core gender-identity that she has a reproductive organ, which in the event of sexual intercourse might produce a pregnancy that will change her body drastically, albeit temporarily, and will also deeply affect her whole life. This profound change takes a different course in the different stages of pregnancy. To start with, as already indicated by Bibring *et al.*, the 'foreign body' will be responsible for an increase of the libidinal concentration of the self, and an early enhanced narcissism which ceases when the quickening appears; the foetus is then experienced as a separate object within the self and this awareness interrupts the pregnant woman's narcissistic process. According to Lester and Notman, this 'quickening initiates the earliest contact with the infant and thus signals the awakening of motherliness in the

mother . . . that is the urge to nurture and care for the infant'
(1986, p. 364). 'The child will always remain part of herself,
and at the same time will always have to remain an object that
is part of the outside world and part of her sexual mate'
(Bibring *et al.*, p. 16). Clearly these concepts apply if pregnancy
is regarded as a developmental phase in a maturational process
and as an essential part of growth. However, we should be
aware of pathological outcomes, as D. Pines has pointed out,
especially when considering the first pregnancy. After all, these
changes in the body and the mental representations of self,
object, and object-relationships are bound to alter forever the
pregnant woman's view of herself (Pines, D., 1972). 'Once an
adolescent you cannot become a child again; once menopausal
you cannot bear children again; and once a mother you cannot
be a single unit again' (Bibring *et al.*, p. 13).

For women the act of making love takes on a different
dimension than for men since the former are much more aware
than the latter of using the same organ for sexual pleasure as for
procreation. The indescribable richness which is created when a
man and a woman make love beautifully may come home in a
particularly poignant way to a woman. Several women — not
only my patients — have told me of their certainty during
coitus of the most blissful kind that they had just conceived.
The timing of birth has borne out their sudden feeling that the
communication of bodies and emotions was so complete that
the only fitting and natural outcome was a baby. This is a deep
feminine instinct, for even barren women have told me of their
conviction that had they been able to conceive they would have
done so at some particular moment which was the climax of a
perfect sexual union. Such is — or can be — women's
awareness of their bodies and their mental representations.

This awareness grounds them in the reality principle in a
much more biological–psychological way than men who, in
this context, are more prone to the pleasure principle.
Women's drives are object-seeking; as a result some women are
led to certain perverse designs which are alien to men. Some
women get pregnant in the belief that this is the only way to
achieve security with a man, even when the man has asserted his
wish not to be part of this process. For others, the wish to be

SEXUALITY
AND THE
FEMALE BODY

pregnant is born of a desire to inflict revenge on a man they have learnt to hate because they have been deeply humiliated.

I remember an ex-patient of mine, a woman of thirty-one who sought professional help because of severe depression associated with complete frigidity and feelings of revulsion about sex. She also had compulsive morbid fantasies about her daughter who had died at the age of one. All these symptoms had started after she became pregnant with her daughter. Three years before she had fallen in love and begun a relationship with an intelligent and successful man, who to start with was extremely kind to her, but soon began to be sadistic and to beat her. She felt unable to defend herself in an open way. Instead, she resorted to secret monologues, which were a precursor to sexual intercourse and gave her some bitter comfort.

If only I could get pregnant by him, he would have to learn then who is in control, and he'd have to respect me, since I'd be carrying his child. I hate him, but I don't want to show it. I want to hurt him really deeply and I know this would be the best way since he won't be able to get rid of me.

These compulsive ruminations aroused her sexually and she was able to derive a great sense of erotic pleasure and to achieve momentary relief from her anxiety, although as soon as sexual intercourse was over she was filled with self-disgust. Here we see at work an element of revenge coupled with a compulsive libidinal repetitive action which includes a quick switch from ego-syntonic to ego-dystonic, major indicators of perversion. In other words, the action which is first experienced as being compatible with the ego's demands becomes antagonistic to the self after its execution, and it is followed by feelings of remorse and guilt. In women these actions are concretely directed to a self, to an object, and to an object-relationship.

There may be a confusion in the professional literature, as well as in the minds of these women, between femininity, sexuality, and motherhood. They of course derive from the fundamental psychobiological facts of womanhood.

MOTHER,
MADONNA,
WHORE   *What matters is not only the anatomy but also the mental*

representation: the meaning of man or woman is the experience of a psychic structure which operates as such. This representation could be envisaged in great dependency on physiology or, dialectically speaking, on physiological and social factors. Freud's categories – castration complex, woman's castration, penis-envy, phallic stage, unawareness of the vagina, analogy of clitoris with the penis, viewing it as a masculine organ, child as a penis-substitute, clitoral masculine orgasm, active masculine sexuality, passive feminine sexuality – all these categories lead to a synthesis between biology and psychology from which female sexuality is understood. The cultural-sociological factors are absent or appear merely as a secondary influence. Hence, the synthesis is a mechanistic one instead of a dialectic one. (Arnaiz, Puget and Siquier, 1983, pp. 33–4)

This statement goes beyond the merely anatomical dimension and embodies a symbolism that goes deeper than the surface. According to these authors, 'even with the arrival of M. Klein's theories which challenge the phallocentred theories, the female psychic structure appears in a dialectical way with a mother who before anything else is a breast, therefore centred in the nurturing bond and pregnancy. The woman, then, is understood from a mammalian ecological viewpoint' (pp. 33–4, my translation).

A patient told me of her hatred of her body, and how repelled she felt at even the idea of being touched by her husband. During sexual intercourse she would only allow him to penetrate her, and then she felt at peace; she had never experienced pleasure from foreplay. During her pregnancies she had felt content with her body and proud of it. It was as if she had never experienced her body as belonging to herself for her own pleasure, but only as a 'bridge' either for the man's sexual release or for her functioning as a pregnant woman.

Bleichmar points out how 'the castration complex in the girl orientates and normalizes sexual desire but not the gender, which has social values and connotations. In other words, it will basically decide the organization of the female sexuality but not its femininity' (1985, p. 27, my translation).

Whereas men's intellectual achievements are viewed as

consistent with their gender, women in parallel situations sometimes find themselves in conflict, not only with the successful use of their intellects (something often held to be the prerogative of the man's world), but also with their own femininity, which is often interlinked with the use of their bodies. At these times women experience a splitting process in relation to their intellects and their femininity. This is especially so for women whose mothers have not used their own intellectual capacities, sometimes because of socio-economic pressures which do not affect their daughters. Such a woman will fear success, believing that not only men but also her internal mother will retaliate against her for her achievements. This can result in an extreme exaggeration, arising from underrating of the intelligence while equating an overrating of the female body with femininity. Some professional women who come for therapy have considerable intellectual standing and have reaped concomitant financial rewards. Men in equal positions would find it easy to boast about their successes, but these women had difficulties in acknowledging them, and when they did it was with embarrassment and disbelief. It is as if they felt in open rebellion against the traditional standards. In the course of their professional and social lives, and despite themselves, they experience a mixed response when sexually approached by unattractive and uninteresting men. On the one hand they feel humiliated and angry, but on the other, they feel secretly reassured and flattered by such unwanted approaches. Such is the bitter power that the female body and femininity have been assigned as opposed to the lack of power accorded to a woman's intellect.

In this context, one patient came for therapy because of her difficulties in achieving a high professional standard, despite her outstanding accomplishments as a student. During her therapy she talked about her inability to see herself functioning simultaneously as a woman and as a successful professional. She then explained how she had overcome her disgust about sexual intercourse when she began to 'talk dirty'. By this she meant that she would describe to her lover fantasies about how a strange, 'tarty and smelly' woman was seducing him. This she would do in story-telling style, very slowly, using obscene words and filthy scenarios. The 'dirtier' it all got the more excited she would become, and eventually she would have an orgasm imagining her partner with another woman. This was accompanied by her being actually chained to the bed, completely immobilized and utterly subservient to her partner. Afterwards she would find the whole exercise appalling and would feel depressed and unworthy of any tenderness or love.

During therapy it became apparent that this woman's fantasies had to do with an uncaring and neglectful mother who had made a very profitable marriage to a man she deeply despised. My patient was unable to feel deserving of any man's love, and she would conjure up the fantasy of her mother and identify with her during sexual intercourse. Such was the degree of identification that she would split herself into two women who were populating her from within. One of them was seen by her as a despicable creature who could experience orgasm when denigrated by 'making hate' instead of making love; the other was a professional scholar who would belittle and undermine men while unable to get satisfaction from any intimate relationships with them. Professional success was unconsciously linked with killing her mother. The latter was literally experienced by her as an 'internal saboteur' who would undermine all her efforts to succeed. We can clearly see in this patient the splitting between her 'libidinal ego' and the 'internal saboteur' described by Fairbairn (1944). According to his theories, the baby adopts this mechanism when she has been faced with maternal failure. On this point, as Sayers (1986, p. 65) has reminded us, Fairbairn returns to Horney's later theories (Horney, 1939) of the girl's Oedipus complex in which she claims that incestuous attachment in the child occurs only when the parents are so wrapped up in their own interests that they neglect those of the child.

Lasch calls attention to Reich's description of women whose mothers had treated them as surrogates for an absent or unsatis-factory husband. They reported fantasy-wishes, traceable to early childhood, to be used as mother's missing phallus. One woman, an actress, claimed to have a feeling of euphoria while being admired by the audience: ' "intense excitement experienced over the *entire body surface and a sensation of*

26   *standing out, erect, with her whole body.* Obviously," Reich
adds, *"she felt like a phallus with her whole body"* ' (1984, p.
171 n., author's italics).

It is easier and perhaps more conventional to believe in the
use of the female body as a symbolic phallus than to view the
female body and its symbolism as a complete and different
version of the male body. But why should a woman's body
become a phallus in fantasy — why should it not instead
represent important, complex, and uniquely feminine physical,
physiological, and symbolic characteristics? It may have been
convenient to hold the former view in order to preserve and
perpetuate male superiority. Thus, man is believed to possess
the phallus as a symbol of all power which women are not
allowed to have, except in a vicarious and artificial way, by
psychologically and even 'anatomically' transplanting themselves as men in disguise. In my view the mothers described by
Annie Reich were suffering from this phenomenon, seeing
themselves as inferior to men and, in their own generation,
unable to develop their own sense of self and intellect with all
their complexities. They were acquiescing in a master model
based on male superiority.

Times are changing and so are freedom and choice.
However, some women who know that their mothers relied on
their female bodies to give men sexual gratification, and on
their capacity for procreativity to secure a position of power in
a man's world, have a deep dread of challenging those old
principles. These women are in constant fear that their mothers
will envy their own academic and intellectual achievements
which they, their mothers, rarely had access to. This 'success
anxiety' in women could become the equivalent of castration
anxiety which earlier writers had ascribed to women. The
mother now becomes the 'internal saboteur' which is felt to
repress other accomplishments.

Women's bodies are designed to accommodate another
living body. But the wonder is more than the static situation,
marvellous though it is, of one body within another. The fact
that the inner body is growing within the outer one is

MOTHER,
MADONNA,
WHORE

impossible to ignore, however disturbing or unwelcome it may
be to the mother. Indeed, many women express strong feelings

only gratified when pregnant.

Pregnancy concentrates the mind on reality. It has often been said that female sexuality remains 'a riddle', and that this might have to do with women's sexual organs being 'hidden away', making the subject obscure. Certainly this argument loses part of its power if one attempts to apply it to the changes in the female reproductive organs during pregnancy. These changes are so manifest that they give rise to powerful feelings in both males and females. Breasts and uterus swell and change. Not only do the breasts have a nurturing function, they also are a focus of sexual stimulus, called by Freud (1905) an 'organ pleasure', in other words they are capable of producing sexual pleasure without necessarily having any direct link to a vital function. This is very well known to the father-to-be, who frequently comments that as soon as the baby is born he will be deprived of all goodies from the maternal/libidinal breast because the baby will be taking it away from him. Incidentally, many women can experience vaginal orgasm simply by the caressing and sucking of their breasts by their sexual partner.

In some women any sexual pleasure related to their breasts ceases not only in pregnancy, but for years after weaning has occurred. This phenomenon has been described to me by many women who experience a tremendous sense of loss when they renew lovemaking with their partners and become aware of this missing dimension that had previously afforded them such erotic excitement. Some of them had breast-fed their babies for up to two years; some had found this sexually gratifying but not always. They thought it possible that with the arrival of the baby, an important part of their bodies had been made redundant as a site of sexual stimulation, and that their right to this pleasure had been superseded by the new function, so much more vital in its central role in the nurturing of their offspring.

It is extremely difficult to differentiate femininity from the function of motherhood, perhaps because its nature is so deeply intertwined with emotional, physical, biological, hormonal, cultural, sociological, and physiological factors that are exclusively associated with womanhood. For women, as for men, orgasm can have a variety of bodily and mental representations; but the fact that women's bodies accommodate the enlarged male sexual organ, as well as, potentially, the growing foetus during pregnancy, for them adds a completely new dimension.

Many psychoanalysts, from very early on, have researched the subject of orgasm. I will mention only a few. Ferenczi talks about the phallus and vagina as cosmic symbols, not by reference to myths but by his interpretations of embryological, physiological, and psychological facts. He develops the view that all life is determined by a tendency to return to the womb, something very apparent in the sexual act. The sexual development of the individual culminates in the primacy of the genital zone, which is achieved by a process leading from autoerotism via narcissism to genital object-love. There is no part of the organism which is not represented in the genitalia, so that in coitus sexual tension is discharged on behalf of the entire organism. He puts forward the theory that 'the mutual attraction is nothing but the expression of the fantasy of veritably merging one's self with the body of the partner or perhaps of forcing one's way *in toto* into it (as a substitute for the mother's womb)' (1924, p. 34). Once more we could see how his theory could apply to the man, but not to the woman. As Chasseguet-Smirgel points out, 'Ferenczi finds himself obliged to write of an identification by the woman with the man's penis in coitus in order to ensure a symmetrical satisfaction for both sexes of the desire to return to the mother's womb' (1985b, p. 33). D. Pines makes an illuminating comment on this topic:

In my experience there is at times a universal wish to return to the safety of the mother's womb. A man may fulfil this wish unconsciously when he penetrates his sexual partner's body, in fantasy his mother's, and can feel satisfied and satisfactory to her. This experience in his adult life may do much to repair the wounds of childhood. A woman's body can only enable her to do so when she concretely becomes a mother herself and can identify both with her mother and herself as a child. (1986, p. 7)

MOTHER,
MADONNA,
WHORE

A woman author friend of mine, while reading the manuscript

of this book, made the following remark: 'I once asked a large number of men this question: "When you see a pregnant woman, who do you identify with?" Almost all said "The baby". Can you imagine *any* woman saying that?'

Female patients have told me of how they experience orgasm, and even conception, as a symbolic invasion of their vagina by a baby during sexual intercourse with their partner. Many women have talked of having fantasies that during sexual intercourse with a partner a baby is coming into their vagina; they have felt protective and caring towards that particular partner because he was experienced as a baby returning to the womb. This appears to be reciprocated in men's fantasies during intercourse. I remember a woman patient who told me about her latest lover's request while in the act of making love: 'I want to get all my body inside your cunt.' My patient continued, 'I felt terrified, it was as if this man's body would have become like a baby's and he wanted to get back into mother's body, but it was my own body'.

According to Lemoine-Luccioni (1982), pregnancy and labour for a woman are the equivalent of sexual intercourse for a man. Moreover:

During sexual intercourse the man looks in the woman for the Other, but he finds his mother, which arouses in him an archaic libido, from before the sexualization and the differentiation of the sexes, where he loses his sexuality. The woman seeks in the man the paternal and omnipotent phallus, to find instead only a weak penis. The woman, then, in order to preserve the paternal phallic fantasies, falls into the maternal function and becomes phallic. (p. 39, my translation)

Why is it so difficult to view men and women in a symmetrical way? If we make the attempt, we can envisage the following parallel situation in both sexes. The little boy envies his father's capability to have an intimate sexual relationship with his mother because the father takes away from him his first object-relationship whom he desires in all ways, including sexually. The boy is left in a position in which he envies and hates his father and fears his own projective feelings of father's retaliation, even to castration.

The little girl is equally envious of her mother enjoying an intimate sexual relationship with her father, which, furthermore, can create a new being growing within her mother's body. The little girl's envy has to do with mother's capacity to be pregnant, and her fears correspond to her own projective feelings of her mother's retaliation making her barren or incapable of procreation; that would be equivalent to the fear of being castrated (Klein, 1928, 1932, 1933, 1935, 1955). Thus there is a symmetrical situation for boys and girls with their adult equivalents, to deny which is to deny the differentiation of the sexes. Every theory aimed at understanding these phenomena through one gender only will create misunderstandings.

The problem, though, is the change of sexual object in the girl. As Bleichmar (1985) points out, the question concerns not only to change from mother to father, but also why the little girl should wish to be a girl in a paternalistic, masculine, and phallic world. Mitchell poses a similar and important question when she says:

The girl has another story to learn. Her love of her mother is not, like the boy's, culturally dangerous, just sexually 'unrealistic' within the terms of the culture. If she persists in the belief that she has a penis . . . she will be disavowing reality and this will be the basis of a future psychosis. In the 'ideal' case she will recognize her phallic inferiority, identify with the mother to whom she is to be compared, and then want to take her place with her father. (1984, p. 231)

I very much agree with Kohon that 'independently of the sex of the child — what counts is the threat of the loss of the mother' (1984, p. 78). In the psychoanalytical literature most authors have acknowledged this fact. It is especially relevant for perverse psychopathology, in which faulty pre-oedipal phases — the oral and anal phases — account for more perverse behaviour than was previously thought. Sperling stresses the point when she acknowledges that: 'The childhood fetish represents a pathological defence against separation from mother on the oral and anal levels: it seems that separation anxiety due to loss of the pre-oedipally gratifying mother is of greater importance than castration anxiety' (1963, p. 391).

Nevertheless, psychotherapists tend to go for the traditional theories of the girl's libidinal development, which are based on the boy's. It seems to me that we have stuck to the theory of the girl's penis-envy in order to deny an unconscious awareness of mothers' unparalleled power over their infants in the early pre-oedipal phase.

It is not good enough, as Kohon claims, to invoke an equivalent 'womb-envy' applicable to men. Indeed, as he says, 'instead of trying to explain the differences of the sexes, this concept would do away with the differences' (p. 79). In Mitchell's words, 'So long as we reproduce ourselves as social beings through a heterosexual relationship, human society must distinguish between the sexes . . . For human society to exist at all, men and women must be marked as different from each other' (1980, pp. 234–5).

Let us first try to assess this differentiation and then deal with the peculiarities in each case. Male and female libidinal developments are different, as are their psychopathological aspects. In descriptions of male perversions, there is often the underlying assumption that there is a 'universal belief of children that the mother has a phallus, *not in the existence of a real penis in the father*' (Kohon, p. 79, author's italics). I wonder whether, when we talk about this 'imaginary maternal phallus/breast', we are really referring to a 'breast/phallus' which exerts a controlling power that mothers could harness to guide their young infants' lives?

In this context I am grateful to Zilbach (1987) for her original and most illuminating ideas. She challenges Freudian theories of the development of sexuality in the girl, especially in relation to the phallic stage, and offers an alternative female equivalent of the masculine concept of the phallus. She believes that the primary core femininity in the girl starts to become established very early on, in identification with her mother, and contains the wish for a baby as a potential creation. Later on, in reaching adulthood, actual procreation will start deeply within a woman when the sperm is 'actively engulfed', and not passively received as previously thought. This 'active engulf- ment' is the core, the beginning, and the growing essence of being female. The potential for creation by active engulfment is non-conflictual and non-oedipal, and it constitutes the base from which many later psychological steps are taken along the path to womanhood. In Zilbach's view the genital phase is not the end of the separate developmental line for females, for there are subsequent stages, menarche, pregnancy, and so on; these stages could also benefit from re-analysis in the light of her theory.

In my own clinical experience, women sometimes seem able to perceive their bodies in a whole way only when they are being penetrated during sexual intercourse. Their vagina becomes alive and they are now certain that there is an organ which responds in a complementary way to the Other. This feeling is again present during labour. According to the old tales, as Lemoine-Luccioni (1982) has reminded us, pregnancy not only brings a baby but also sometimes energizes a vaginal orgasm and, so the myth goes on, procreation can cure frigidity.

Kubie (1974), in 'The drive to become both sexes', describes a process by which man and woman alike are unconsciously seeking either to supplement or to complement their own gender with the opposite one. The more unconscious is this drive, the more self-destroying it becomes and the more influential it is in determining basic activities in life, ranging from choice of partner to professional pursuits. This process, however, is always doomed to end in failure and to produce deep frustration, since the unconscious, desired goal is never realized. Kubie goes on to speculate that, for some, the goal of sexual intercourse is neither orgasm nor reproduction but a process of 'magical change'. Hence 'post coitum tristum' may have to do with the realization that this need for transmutation into dual gender through sexual intercourse is unattainable. Kubie expands on the implications, especially the deep repercussions this drive produces in the lack of commitment these individuals experience in their daily lives, a source of much suffering for them. Again, he refers to the symbolic and unconscious needs rather than biophysical or biochemical requirements, which are misrepresented by unconscious oral symbols and therefore become insatiable. The penis has been unconsciously equated with a frustrated breast, therefore becoming incapable of affording sexual satisfaction, but offering instead further frustrations.

This insatiability (the unfulfilment of the impossible) is related to the fact that human beings so often make hate in bed under the illusion that they are making love, and how often and how tragically even the full physiological gratification of sexual craving leads not to a sense of fulfilment but to sadness, terror, and anger, and most important of all to its immediate and incessant repetition. (p. 417)

He adds that there is no possible escape and no rest since the immediate orgasmic fulfilment has become a transient betrayal — an illusion — because it merely triggers off a recurrence of the need. We can identify in his findings many of the characteristics of perverse behaviour. He also notes in the same paper that at some point it will be necessary to consider how the partial components of the drive to become both sexes could be related to disturbances such as exhibitionistic behaviour, transvestitism, overt homosexuality, eating anomalies, and kleptomania. It seems to me that he is describing two different processes. In the 'magical change' there is neither pleasure nor procreation, merely the illusion of apprehending both sexes, with a resulting gender neutrality. However, when he refers to 'making hate' he certainly describes the basic nature of perversions, which is embodied in the predicament of many of my ex-patients (see p. 22).

In female perversion not only the whole body but also its mental representations are used to express sadism and hostility. Women express their perverse attitudes not only through but also towards their bodies, very often in a self-destructive way. If we look at the psychopathologies most frequently associated with women, we find syndromes of self-injury associated with biological or hormonal disorders affecting the reproductive functioning. Such is the case with anorexia nervosa, bulimia,

34 and forms of self-mutilation, where the menses, their absence or their presence, may act as indicators of the severity of the pathological condition. These women experience a feeling of elation from the manipulation of their bodies when they are starving, and which disappears when they start to eat again. They experience a sense of power through being in control of the shapes and forms their bodies assume as a result of the physical injuries and abuse they inflict on themselves.

Perversion in women is not so clearly and exclusively connected with the expression of hostility and release of anxiety through just one organ as it is with men. Neither does it have that fixation so characteristic of men. Perhaps this is the reason why women generally have a better prognosis than men. In women perversion operates fully through their bodies as whole. Irigaray asserts the richness of woman's sexuality thus: 'Woman has sex organs just about everywhere. She experiences pleasure almost everywhere. Even without speaking of the hysterization of her entire body, one can say that the geography of her pleasure is much more diversified, more multiple in its differences, more complex, more subtle, than is imagined-in an imaginary centred a bit too much on one and the same' (1977, p. 103). In my view, these 'multiple pleasure-sources' mentioned by Irigaray can become in perverse women the focus for self-inflicted pain, from which they derive perverse libidinal gratification.

Perhaps my argument will become clearer if I share with you some of the predicaments with which my women patients have entrusted me and which have directed me towards this way of thinking.

A case of 'perverse' cosmetic surgery: Mrs Z came to see me because of 'premenstrual tension' (her own words). She was a very attractive, tall, blonde, slender, and smartly dressed woman who looked much younger than her chronological age of thirty-eight. Her eyes, though, looked rather empty, and her movements were uninhabited by any emotion. Indeed, the perfection of her looks and the absence of blemishes reminded me of a male transvestite. Perhaps this first countertrans-

MOTHER, MADONNA, WHORE ferential reaction should have provided me with a more immediate insight into some of her problems which, in the difficulties in putting them into words.

During the first interview she told me that she felt constantly depressed and that she was 'intensely bothered' by an ever-present sensation which she described as 'being outside myself'. By this she meant that she was aware that she was not fully participating in any given situation, as if neither her mind nor her body belonged to her. She had become, as it were, the witness of her own actions and devoid of any feelings, irrespective of how much they impinged on her life.

She was unable to give me any other relevant information and eventually began to associate her present condition with past events. She believed that her problems had started five years earlier, when she became pregnant by her present husband (her fifth) before their marriage, and he categorically refused to let her go ahead with the pregnancy. She felt hurt but unable to define her own rights, and went along with an abortion both to please him and also because, in the bargain, she gained a promise of marriage. Her husband, a very wealthy man, was at times 'mothering' towards her. Nevertheless, reluctantly, she recalled that the night before the abortion took place he was callous towards her, especially when he refused to caress her breasts because they were 'too big' as a result of her pregnancy. He never showed up at the clinic, and she found it all too painful. Since then she had felt despondent and empty.

To make things worse, three or four months after the start of the relationship, seven years earlier, she had become aware that he was a transvestite. In her absence he had been wearing her clothes. She asked him about it and he admitted to his cross-dressing. He then 'demanded' her participation in these practices. She began to give it, in the belief that it could relieve him of this problem or perhaps diminish its intensity.

Her cooperation produced exactly the opposite response, as he became more and more demanding of her time, perfection, and skills. By now, he wanted to do it every day; this required not only his getting dressed as a female, but also *her* wearing very specific gear, usually extremely tarty. She had to perform several sketches in which she had to play a 'dominant' role, but always according to *his* script. To start with these sketches had been rather benign, but they had become more and more hostile and aggressive in nature, with stiletto shoes, chains, whips, chokers, and so on. She found the whole thing repulsive and had been turned off sex completely.

So far, you might say, this was simply one more case of sadomasochistic behaviour, not so unusual in couples with collusive perverse actions. But what I would like to emphasize here is my patient's massive denial of herself as a whole human being and her utter self-denigration as a woman. She came to consult me under the easy disguise of premenstrual tension, and perhaps half-believed this explanation.

Let me now go to the heart of the matter, which came up much later during treatment. After the abortion and the bargained wedding, a long saga of complaints issued from her husband about her physical looks. First he objected to the size of her nose, and proceeded to 'suggest' a cosmetic operation for which he was only too willing to pay. After she complied with this 'recommendation', he told her that 'perhaps her teeth were not completely right'. She then submitted to extensive dental surgery. After that there were 'bags under my eyes' and eventually he saw her breasts as 'too big'. She not only underwent all these operations acquiescently but, when talking of the last one, she retorted forcefully: 'it had to do with a medical condition', since her breasts were found to have many cysts. The surgeon removed her breasts and filled the empty spaces with silicone; she said that never after the operation had her breasts been sensitive to any erotic stimuli.

This patient, whom I saw a long time ago, exemplifies clearly the speculation put forward by Granoff and Perrier (1980). In explaining the psychopathology of the perverse woman, they say that the splitting of the ego created by cosmetic surgery has deep and everlasting effects on the woman's personality. According to these authors,

the woman becomes a fetish in herself, endowed like all fetishes with sexual significance yet at the same time entirely unsuited to serve the normal sexual aim. Such a woman responds with her fetishistic body to heterosexual relationships as a defence against latent homosexuality. The man is instrumental since he has been rejected by her from the moment he attempts to assume a phallic relationship with her. His firm conviction, stated as 'you are my woman', is linked to his collusive attitude in treating her as a fetish. (p. 80, my translation)

I have observed this complicated mechanism operating in many women patients. During the course of treatment Mrs Z began gradually to assert herself. Then her husband became increasingly worried about this development and 'claimed' to be her 'owner'; he suddenly manufactured a trip abroad which would take her away from an increasing awareness of her own sense of self. I never saw her again. She stopped her process of individuation when she felt that this might endanger her own sense of 'survival'.

Is it surprising that this woman experienced neither her mind nor her body as belonging to herself? Actually they did not. She had massive self-contempt for her own body and shape, and this drove her to act in a perverse and collusive way with her husband. It had taken her many years and five marriages to accomplish her goal, which was to find the 'right' partner for the execution of her revenge against her own gender, and to have her body and mind slaughtered according to *her own unconscious perverse* designs. Her mind had been taken over by this perverse man, who was so obviously sadistic towards women, and her body had been redesigned according to his expectations of what a female body should look like. Nothing had remained of herself that she could acknowledge as such.

Khan can help us to understand this woman's and her husband's perversion when he describes how

the pervert cannot surrender to intimacy and instead retains a split-off, dissociated, manipulative ego-control of the situation. This is both his achievement and failure in the intimate *situation. It is this failure that supplies the compulsion to repeat the process again and again. The nearest that the pervert can come to experiencing surrender is through visual, tactile, and sensory identifications with the other object in the intimate situation in a state of surrender. Hence, though the pervert arranges and motivates the idealization of instinct, he*

38   *himself remains outside the experiential climax.* (1979, pp. 22–3, author's emphasis)

To understand female sexual perversion we shall have to ignore the male version and take a new look; otherwise, conclusions based on comparing female to male perversions become contrived and inaccurate. This, I believe, is the fault in Zavitzianos' (1971) paper on fetishism and exhibitionism in females. Whereas I appreciate the painstaking and almost heroic efforts made by this author, I disagree with his conclusions. I shall try very briefly to demonstrate the reasons for my disagreement.

Zavitzianos describes his patient, Lilian, as suffering from fetishism and exhibitionism. Her masturbating while reading books is interpreted by him as a fetish, replacing not the 'maternal penis (as in the case of male fetishism) but the penis of the father' (p. 302). This started when Lilian was three, after her brother's birth, when she was moved out of her parents' bedroom. Her exhibitionistic behaviour also started when she was a young girl, when she would walk around naked and play with her genitalia, surprising those around her. She had also begun stealing, first money from her mother's wallet and later other items that she liked and were useful to her. This was done in a skilful and careful manner. Both the use of books and her exhibitionism, which she enacted from inside her father's car as an adult, reappeared while she was in analysis after her delinquency stopped, and masturbation was resumed. It seems to me that this reappearance had to do with a deep regression to an oral phase representing her primitive wish to merge with her mother/analyst.

My own speculation is that the books would symbolize her mother's breasts, which brought her much relief, dispelled her loneliness and helped her to fall asleep. Her exhibitionism from within her father's car had some womb-like qualities which afforded her safety and a sense of containment, similar also to the analyst's consulting room.

MOTHER, MADONNA, WHORE

Notwithstanding my difference of opinion, I strongly agree with Zavitzianos' diagnosis of Lilian as suffering from perversion. However, I believe that her perversion was not an

equivalent to perversions found in males: it was instead
intrinsically female. Not only her psychopathological symptoms but also her early background confirm my diagnosis.
'Lilian very much wanted to have children of her own,'
Zavitzianos reports, 'yet she neglected and mistreated those
who happened to be temporarily in her care. It was a source of
real pleasure to hurt them, usually by poking or pinching them,
often to the point of producing bruises. She would also
masturbate the little boys, and hug (but not masturbate) the
little girls, in her charge' (p. 298). He goes on: 'Lilian's mother
was also a psychopathic personality, with a behaviour pattern
identical to Lilian's. Her relationship with the patient was on a
narcissistic and symbiotic basis. She selfishly and jealously kept
her away from the father. She had been using her daughter to
satisfy vicariously her own delinquent strivings.' He also
mentions that 'she was physically overstimulated by being
masturbated in infancy' (p. 299), though it is not very clear as
to whether she was stimulated by mother or father, but it
appears as if the latter was responsible. However, I would
suspect that she was also subjected to sexual seduction by her
mother. Here we can see the mechanisms of female perversion
at work: while playing a 'maternal role', she was doing to
others what had been inflicted upon her at an early age. Her
mother also corresponds to my description of perverse motherhood. Lilian's exhibitionistic behaviour is similar to my
exhibitionistic patient who was sexually abused by her mother
(and whose full clinical account is given in Chapter 5). I believe
that Lilian was yearning for an early pre-oedipal love/hate
relationship with her 'narcissistic and psychopathic' mother, of
whom she felt deprived, at the age of three, when her brother
was born.

Zavitzianos also claims that his patient's delinquent
behaviour was due partly to complete suppression of masturbation. Here again we note his firm adherence to the
equivalence of female and male sexuality. In this respect it is
relevant to quote Laufer's statement that 'the assumption [is]
often made that female masturbation has the same normal
significance as masturbation for the male' (1982, p. 301). She
sees that for some women the avoidance of the use of the hand

40   for masturbation is a differential characteristic between male and female sexuality. She then develops the hypothesis that the little girl unconsciously identifies her hand with that of her mother's, and that the quality of the relationship between mother and daughter will determine the latter's attitudes towards masturbation at different stages. In the pre-oedipal phase, if the girl feels unable to identify with her mother because of her inability to produce babies she would experience the activity of her hand as a source of anxiety. During adolescence, if she hates her mother's sexual body and is unable to identify with her and her body, the adolescent girl will use her hand to attack her own body in a compulsive way by, for example, cutting her wrists or arms. These activities, according to Laufer, occur as a consequence of 'an outburst of uncontrolled hostility against the mother, the sexual partner, or the analyst' (p. 298). I have observed exactly the same sequences in women who 'indulge' in compulsive shoplifting, which I consider can be female perverse behaviour, as explained by Greenacre (1953a).

The problems of these women are related to their gender and implicitly to their reproductive functions. In doing such harm to their bodies they are expressing tremendous dissatisfaction, not only with themselves but also with their mothers, who provided them with the bodies against which they are now fighting. The power that motherhood conveys can scarcely be overemphasized; it is a theme to which I shall return in Chapter 4.

My present point, however, is that the reproductive functions and organs are used by both sexes to express perversion. Perverse men use their penises to attack and show hatred towards symbolic sources of humiliation, usually represented by part-objects. If perversion in the man is focused through his penis, in the woman it will similarly be expressed through her reproductive organs. While man pursues his perverse goals with his penis, woman does so with her whole body, since her reproductive organs are much more widespread and their manifestations are more apparent.

The power of the womb distinguishes women from men and leads to the power of motherhood — truly as potent as, and usually more far-reaching and more pervasive than, the power of money or law or social position. It is a form of power which may take years or even generations to become fully manifest, and it is rarely reversible. It is a power which is normally used in a beneficent way, but the same instincts that produce love, fulfilment, and security can, if things go wrong, produce their opposites. The power of the womb can lead to perversions, as I shall describe in the next chapter.

3 THE POWER OF THE WOMB

T HE STUDY of some of the characteristics of the female libido and of other features which are exclusive to the female inner world might help us to understand the aetiology of perversion in women. We might then no longer see female perversions as parallels to the psychopathology found in men, and come to recognize their own separate and basic causes.

The essential point lies in women's capacity for procreation, the expression of which is fundamentally different from anything men experience. This capacity drastically affects not only women's emotional lives, but also the mental representations of their bodies and, concretely, their physical bodies, albeit for a fixed period of time. With this as a starting point, we need to understand at least two different but interrelated phenomena if we are to make hypotheses about female sexual perversions.

One phenomenon concerns 'inner space', a term used by Erikson (1968) to describe not only pregnancy and childbirth, but also lactation and all parts of the female anatomy associated with fullness, warmth, and generosity. According to

MOTHER,
MADONNA,
WHORE

him, the inner space has greater actuality than that of the 'missing organ', the penis. As he was able to show in his research at the University of California, boys and girls use space differently. Whereas boys most frequently use outer space, girls emphasize inner space. Thus, the two sexes are different in their 'experience of the ground plan of the human body' (p. 273). Erikson goes on to say that 'in female experience an "inner space" is at the centre of despair even as it is the very centre of potential fulfilment' (p. 278). This 'inner space' is related to the feminine core gender-identity and the mental representations of the body.

The second phenomenon concerns time, which is related to rhythmicity and biology. This is 'the biological clock'. It is especially important in adult decisions about motherhood, particularly when 'time is running out'.

This phenomenon can become difficult to bear for some women who have devoted their lives solely to their careers. They have shown determination at the beginning of their adult lives not to have children in order to advance professionally. Women in this group usually come for therapy in their thirties, suffering from increasing anxiety and ambivalence about their long-held conviction of not wanting babies. Now they feel persecuted by time and by the approaching menopause. I have found that this is by no means a rare phenomenon, but it is far from inevitable. Many women when subjected to the pressures of the biological clock nevertheless achieve fulfilled womanhood.

A similar point is being made by Lax when she says: 'Single women in their late thirties frequently feel threatened by the "biological clock". Such women experience the approach of menopause much sooner than women who are in a gratifying relationship and, at this time, their search for a man frequently reaches frantic proportions' (1982, p. 160). She adds that women under these circumstances often engage in unsuitable relationships, and if an abortion has to be carried out because the pregnancy is unwanted a severe depression follows. Lax cites another outcome for this group of women: the surfacing of lesbian impulses as a result of their giving up hope for a mutually loving relationship with a man. Such impulses correspond to a partial psychosexual regression to an early relationship with their mothers. Lax goes on to say: 'these women show no evidence of homosexual panic. This lack of panic is undoubtedly due in part to the present-day relaxation of mores, which also reinforces these women's lesbian rationalization' (p. 160).

There are distinctive areas of anxiety/fulfilment regarding womanhood and motherhood which are expressions of resolution or failure in relation to earlier stages of psychological maturation, and they are subjected to the dictates of the biological clock.

The inner space and the biological clock are different phenomena, but their effects intertwine. In the maturational crises in women's lives sometimes one is more important, sometimes the other. In adolescence the 'inner space' tends to be the more important of the two in relation to fantasies about pregnancy, while later the 'biological clock' can be more dominant. At menopause the two come together. The argument presented in this chapter roughly follows this chronology.

D. Pines makes an important point when she notes the 'marked psychic distinction between the wish to become pregnant and the wish to bring a live child into the world and become a mother' (1982, p. 311). The former comes very early in life. The female core gender-identity includes a pre-oedipal identification with mother which becomes well established by the second year of life, when body awareness and internal representations have become distinct and therefore differentiation between the sexes has been acknowledged. The wish for a baby has become by then part of the 'primary femininity' (Stoller, 1976). This has been widely researched in studies of mothers and babies, taking in the first three months of infant life. Such studies give us access to the object-relationship theory and to assessments of normality and pathology both in little girls' gender-identity and in the functioning of adult women as mothers.

I shall now deal with the characteristics of the feminine core gender-identity and its vicissitudes during the very early phases and during adolescence. I shall present clinical material from the treatment of women who have struggled not only in the achievement of their own gender-identity, but also in the acknowledgement of their children's gender.

In the establishment of the core gender-identity, the object-relationship the baby has with its mother, and her acceptance and acknowledgement of her baby's sex from birth, are crucial. This involves the mother's acceptance of her own gender and her own mental representations, which can sometimes be a difficult and painful process because of her deep unconscious expectations of her future baby's sex in relation to herself.

Boys and girls have very different experience in the formation of their gender-identities. Abelin (1978) believes that while early gender-identity is more easily available to boys, girls tend to establish a 'generational identity'. By this he means the location of the self in the girl between two objects, one bigger than herself — her mother — and one smaller — a symbolic baby: 'I am smaller than mother but bigger than baby' (p. 147). I consider that this generational identity is associated not only with the mirroring of the mother's body in the girl's, but also with the biological clock, which exclusively belongs to the female world. It has been widely noted that boys dis-identify from mothers much earlier than girls. In a parallel way fathers play a more important role in boys' early years of development than in girls'. Indeed, from the very start men are provided with a rich and unique experience denied to women. As infants their first object-relationship is with the opposite sex. This early situation might enable them later on in life to develop a sense of familiarity and ease in their relationships with women, whereas women are distanced from their fathers during the pre-oedipal stage and may consequently experience difficulties in their relationships with men. Certainly this does not mean that boys automatically have an easier life; it all depends on the quality of that early relationship with mother. Some men become caring, tender, sensitive, and responsible, whereas others grow to be exactly the opposite: hating, cruel, sadistic, and insensitive.

Such is the power that women have when they become mothers. Obviously the early experiences do not account for all possible future psychological traits, but certainly they leave a strong impression in all human beings. In this light, let us look at some of the differentiations between the sexes.

Some of these differentiations are concrete features, but others have to do with a wide range of symbolizations which derive from an immense world of fantasy for both sexes. It is true that boys are born with a penis which could symbolically (i.e. in phallic fantasies) give them a sense of power and superiority which women could easily envy. The object of penis-envy is not so much the physical organ as the male position of dominance in the world. I believe this has been overemphasized, and in the process it has been overlooked that women who feel in an inferior position try in a vicarious but vigorous way to achieve their own fantasies of power through their own reproductive organs, and furthermore to act them out. The outcomes of these fantasies range widely, from dreadful to hopeful. The underlying motivations vary from the so-called normal to the very sadistic and cruel. This more extreme motivation is more likely to underlie the fantasies of women who feel degraded, humiliated, and discarded because of their female gender.

Let us start with fantasies about pregnancy. What do these fantasies mean to young, prepubescent girls? At times, conflicts originating very early on in their lives can make them feel undermined, insecure, and in open or hidden rebellion against their mother because they have not been able to achieve a positive female identification. These difficulties surface when they reach puberty.

Young women feel awkward and insecure in dealing with their powerful feelings about the tremendous changes taking place inside and outside their bodies, and sometimes they are not supported by their mothers in their acknowledgement of their sense of femininity. After all, it is well known that while some mothers of adolescent boys show off with them and obtain narcissistic gratification when mistakes are made about their relationship, the same mothers, when in company with attractive adolescent daughters, feel put down and disregarded by the men who make complimentary remarks about their daughters. The fresh beauty of young girls' bodies becomes all the more apparent as their mothers are ageing. A tremendous sense of competition emerges, especially if mothers are approaching the menopause. Again, we are not talking about just one organ, as is the case with boys, who, when they compare themselves with their fathers, may feel inadequate and small; as a result they acknowledge that father is in control. Fathers are rarely in such open competition with their sons. The adolescent boy has an easier transfer of attachment from mother to another woman than does the adolescent girl, since the boy does not need to change his first love-object. The girl, instead, has to make the switch from attachment to mother to attachment to father. If she is then rejected by father she may look for revenge in dreams of pregnancy.

The way a father responds to a daughter's difficulties with her incipient sexuality is important. If he is dismissive and inattentive, the adolescent girl will feel undermined and disparaged; if he is critical and denigrating she will feel devastated. Such feelings can find expression in the typical adolescent rebelliousness, including possibly a compulsive and indiscriminate 'sexual' search, in which the girl's aim is to win recognition of herself and her body. This behaviour has a wide range of mental representations. The girl feels rejected first by mother and then by father. The search is now for both, from one frustrating breast to another breast in the disguise of a penis. However, this primary need presents itself in a 'sexual' disguise because of the overwhelming world of fantasy which is so reinforced and confused by all the secondary sexual characteristics emerging so abruptly at that stage of life. Indeed, each 'sexual' encounter, like each clumsy delinquent action committed by these youngsters, is invested in their minds with both hope and disillusion. Hope disappears very soon and is immediately replaced by intense disappointment since what is sought — a symbolic fusion with mother or, more precisely, with mother's breast and all its inherent nourishing qualities — is never found. They are unaware that this search is for consistent affection. This is concealed not only from themselves, but also from the world, where their rebellious actions meet with so much disapproval and misunderstanding. The reassurance they need is not available from the outside, so they try vicariously to manufacture it from within by means of pregnancy fantasies. At such times, pregnancy becomes incontrovertible proof of belonging to the female gender.

Young girls experience biologically the inner space now ready to be filled, not only with a penis but also with a pregnancy/baby, even if their emotional and psychological equipment is sometimes far too immature to deal with the profound changes of motherhood and their consequences. This partly explains why adolescence is such a vulnerable stage in life. When inadequate and insecure about their femininity they feel no longer able to fantasize about symbolisms attached to the inner space; instead they use their bodies in a concrete way and become pregnant. This is often observed in young delinquent and promiscuous girls.

To understand promiscuity we have to leave aside sexuality and learn about the mental representations of these young women's bodies. These are linked to the frustrating and damaging experiences they have had with their mothers when they were infants. Promiscuity is basically a compulsive, illusory attempt to create object-relationships which is doomed to failure, since the young woman is really flying from a frustrated experience with a mother whom she feels has been unable to nurture her properly. She is now, compulsively and indiscriminately, looking in men for what she missed in her contact with her mother. So, more disappointments are on the way. They are rooted in two different sources: real mother and symbolic father/ mother. Such experiences are extreme cases of a conflict girls face in adolescence. With the awakening of their inner sexuality and the development of their secondary sexual characteristics, their bodies become like their mother's. As a direct consequence, all unresolved early conflicts with mother are revived, especially those related to frustration and anger.

I have had experience of young girls who suffered from this type of problem, for which they were treated at a therapeutic community. While there they had many indiscriminate sexual encounters with rebellious young men, in which it was their secret wish to achieve a degree of intimacy they had never experienced before. These encounters not only were doomed to fail, but also provided the girls with added frustrations. If their quest produced a pregnancy, they were elated since they were

now sure of belonging to the female gender. For some girls the
pregnancy itself was the ultimate achievement and they would
quickly seek an abortion. For others the birth was necessary,
but they would intend to give up the baby as soon as it was born
in the belief they could not take proper care of the new being.
For others still, the pregnancy also offered hope of a closeness
with a growing foetus inside their bodies. At times there was a
sense of triumph, of revenge against their mother. They had
now learnt that their mother's assumed hostile feelings
towards them had not *really* damaged their capacities for
procreation. This is why the mental representation of becoming
a mother is at least a three-generational process: a woman
becomes her mother and her mother's mother. Sometimes, a
feeling of revenge towards their mother or father because of the
way they were treated by them may indicate the kind of future
life the baby boy or girl will have.

Not all authorities would agree with these views. For
example, Limentani says:

Penis-envy can also be a major issue in the case of female
perverts. But, again, is it simply the expression of a longing for
a part of the male anatomy? It could also be that at times it
expresses a deep feeling of frustration at not being able to fulfil
the ambition of giving mother a baby, a symbolic act of
reparation for past fantasy misdeeds. (1987, p. 421)

This view is valid in certain contexts, but my clinical experience has proved to be different, suggesting (as already
indicated) that penis-envy has been overrated. What looks like
this is often in reality quite different: pregnancy offers many
women the chance to inflict a concrete act of revenge on their
mothers, as opposed to a reparation fantasy directed towards
them.

In this context I recall a patient of sixteen who had been
deserted by her young mother at the age of two, when the
mother decided that it was all too much for her. When I saw
her she had been reunited with her mother, with whom she now
had a difficult and bitter relationship for she could not forgive
her mother for having abandoned her so early in life. The

mother herself had been given away by her own mother at her birth. My patient's first reaction when she learnt of her pregnancy was one of delight, saying 'Now my mother will have to put up with my baby.' This girl was so full of rage against her mother that her first pronouncement was 'This will teach my mother.'

Another patient with a similar background, and who experienced her mother as cold and dismissive, responded to her pregnancy by saying 'My mother will kill me.' Clearly she was expressing a hope that her mother would respond in a very emotional way, and thus acknowledge her as a person and woman.

Another fantasy (which, by the way, is common to most women) is related to fears of having a malformed or handicapped baby. The degree of severity of this fantasy is an indicator of a woman's acceptance of her body's capability to produce wonderful or nasty things. In the words of Raphael-Leff, 'Pregnancy, like all *transitional phases*, reawakens earlier unresolved conflicts and anxieties. The archaic clash between her inner imagined life-giving and death-dealing forces is now relocated in the arena of birth, a test, culminating in *proof* of whether she is creative or destructive' (1985, p. 16, author's italics).

These many and varied expectations — of which the future mother may be oblivious — might be present in a potentially dramatic and intense way from her moment of birth. Amongst them are those related to the sex of the baby to be born. Sometimes there are emotional residues from having given birth to a baby of one sex or the other.

At times a sense of bewilderment overrides all other feelings about the sex of the expected child. Such was the predicament of a pregnant patient of mine who said, 'I shall be disappointed by both: by a boy because I don't really have any common interests, especially when I see pictures of nine-year-old boys with football gear; by a girl because such a high value is placed in English society on having a boy.' She continued:

There is only one nephew in the family and it's disgusting how the whole family spends hours about which school he should go

to. He is only aged three. In the meantime his sister is about to
go to college and nobody gives a damn about her. I was
suddenly infused with an enormous sense of relief that I had no
brother, only sisters. Otherwise we should have been treated
very badly.

Bearing in mind the distinction between the desire for
pregnancy and the desire for motherhood, let us examine the
most usual, benign expectations that women have in connection
with becoming mothers. Their fears of motherhood sometimes
run side by side with a tremendous sense of power in
procreativity. When they are ready for procreation their dreams
and fantasies may materialize in the most intimate relationship
with a baby of either sex, such is the degree of emotional
intimacy and physical dependency that women can create in
any new human being, regardless of sex. This early dependency
on women can leave not only physical but also emotional
marks. Only women can have such early and decisive influences
on their offspring, but this monopoly is possible only when
they have reached maturity in their reproductive functions.
Before this, women (or girls, rather) — who are liable to suffer
many frustrations as a result of their early experiences — are
susceptible to strong feelings of envy which may develop into
terrifying sentiments of revenge. They may be led to manufacture vengeful dreams in which they can be as good as boys,
and sometimes better in their own fields. Girls usually have
fantasies of procreation played out with their dolls, friends and
siblings in which they behave either as good mothers or as
nasty, ugly surrogate mothers. We are all familiar with such
situations in fairy tales, and we are now beginning to notice
them in the daily lives of unfortunate families.

Let us think just in female terms for a minute. Within the
female body is that male body which, according to traditional
psychoanalytical views, arouses in women feelings of envy,
competition, and rivalry. In their maternal role women
experience a sense of bewilderment and intense excitement
about having baby boys. After all, they are containing within
themselves the wonders of the opposite sex. In some, a secret
wish to produce a baby boy might be associated with feelings of

accomplishment, because their mother did not give birth to one. I remember a patient of mine talking of the delivery of her son and saying 'When I heard that it was a baby boy I felt completely at peace. My mother, who has three daughters, looked at me and angrily said "How dare you? How dare you?" '

Another patient, whose baby was the first boy in three generations, first reacted with much pride and a sense of fulfilment, but this was soon to give way to an uneasy feeling. She told me how baffled she felt when she realized that she had begun to address him as a 'she', and had a compulsive urge to buy for him very 'feminine' clothes. This was her attempt to pacify fantasied envious attacks on her by her mother, grandmother, and sisters. In other words, her sense of accomplishment had to be covered up by disguising her baby's gender in order to feel safe.

For some, the sense of fulfilment has to do with being intermingled with a male body, to which sex the woman unconsciously wanted to belong. In contrast, other women have misgivings about being 'contaminated in their femininity by maleness' (Raphael-Leff, 1985, p. 16). Some express openly a wish for a son; but others are extremely secretive about it and profess a need for nobody else to know about this 'secret wish'. I have often had such a secret revealed to me by ardent feminists who did not want their 'sisters' to know about it. What does it mean for a woman to contain in her own body the other sex? Such feelings are transmitted after birth and can prevail for a long time. In this way, the attitude of the mother of a baby boy is a key influence on how her son will develop into manhood.

Let us turn now to the woman having a baby girl. We could say that girls too have a unique experience in having their first object-relationship with their own gender. From the moment a baby girl is born, her mother sees a miniature version of herself, a woman, as she mothers her daughter. In normal circumstances this produces a deep feeling of connectiveness and loving security (Zilbach, 1987). But problems arise from the re-enactment of motherhood. The mother's attitude towards the development of her little girl is influenced by how she feels towards her own mother, the body her mother provided her with, and the way she felt accepted or rejected by her mother as a child in her own gender. Thus, the birth of a girl might evoke in the mother the same response her own birth created in her own mother.

Another patient felt disgusted by her pregnancy and had fantasies of becoming such a 'bad mother' that she would neglect her baby, even to the point of letting him die. She was sure that she would be incapable of breast-feeding him since she thought that it was a terrible thing to do to her body. In telling me her history she represented herself as the first child. It was plain that she had felt confused about her feminine identity, and she had had some homosexual affairs during adolescence. When the baby was born she felt bewildered, but simultaneously rather 'brave' in attempting to do 'the right thing'. There she was, breast-feeding her baby, and to her immense surprise even enjoying the mothering process. She said, 'I feel so relieved that a boy was born, I now know that he will be able to distance himself from me. Becoming independent will be an easier task for him than if I had had a girl.' Then she proceeded to tell me for the first time that she remembered her mother telling her that, before she was born, an older sister had died at the age of two months because her mother had been unable to cope with the demands, especially in relation to feeding. This patient had never been able to fantasize about the sex of the future child, such was her terror of causing the death of a baby girl because of her 'fate'. Her own mother was also a second child, but a first-surviving child, and her maternal grandmother had had the same history, her own elder sister having died at the age of three months. This had all been blocked off in my patient's consciousness, but unconscious memories preyed on her during pregnancy.

This case shows how a woman's conflicts about her own gender can result in perverse or perverting attitudes which may well be traceable across at least three generations. If the young mother has from birth been the object of her parents' disappointment for being a girl, and if this parental attitude persists for long, it will almost automatically provoke in her a sense of intense dislike and hatred towards her own body.

54 Nevertheless, she may eventually overcome these feelings and consequently accept her own role as a mother.

Most of what I have described so far relates to the 'inner space'. Now let us turn to the 'biological clock'. There is a wide and spectacular difference in the sense of temporality in males and females. Women have a biological clock that is present from the moment they are born. From menarche to menopause, this clock dominates a woman's lifespan and subjects her to the hope/dread of pregnancy. This grounds women firmly in the reality principle. Not only do they have a different libidinal development from men, but they also experience a feeling of urgency provided by their sense of the inexorable passage of time which is exclusive to their sex and is intimately related to their reproductive functions. The fixed period of nine months for pregnancy makes women especially aware of time and reality, but not necessarily when they are actually pregnant. The many physical changes that take place during pregnancy concentrate the mind and help to make women much more aware than men of important events in life related to their gender-identity, hormones, and reproductive organs. This could be partly responsible for differences in abnormal sexuality between the sexes. This 'biological inexorability' is an overwhelming and irresistible fact and could be responsible for the marked psychological differences between men and women.

Adolescence provides us all with a second chance, an opportunity to mend the damage of traumatic events in early infancy. However, if circumstances are against us things can be much more difficult, especially in gender issues. In girls, adolescence can have serious and drastic effects even when there is no history of previous traumatic experiences. As we shall see when we come to look at the background of a particular ex-patient of mine, the pubescent female body struggles to find expression for its own gender under adverse circumstances which could have undermined it.

The first menstrual period — the menarche — heralds the girl-woman's fecundity. Subsequently she will have periods every four weeks — the menses — which are a constant reminder of her hope/dread of it. They will remain for years to come, yet those years are limited. Hence, ambivalence about becoming a mother will in some cases be associated with a great deal of anxiety that increases as the years go by. Side-effects such as a kind of 'mini-mourning' may follow menstrual periods; the woman feels bereft of the experience of pregnancy, even if she has herself chosen not to become a mother for the time being.

When time is pressing priorities can change. The biological clock is also set to trigger the end of the reproductive functions — menopause. This is sometimes greeted with relief and a sense of peace, but most women experience a tremendous sense of loss; they feel devalued and sense a lowering of self-esteem. Sometimes this corresponds to gender-frustrations encountered during the adolescent period.

That was the case with a professional woman of thirty-one whom I saw some few years ago when she had unexpectedly begun to feel under extreme pressure because she was unable to make up her mind whether to become a mother or not. Earlier, a decision had been made not to have children. The present conflict was being aggravated by the fact that she had fallen in love with another professional, and there was nothing to prevent them from being together and starting a family. She was in the 'unfortunate' predicament of not being able to blame outside circumstances for her feeling of pressure.

All seemed to have been fairly normal from the beginning of her life. Her birth had been much welcomed by both parents. She was the second child in a family of two; her brother was three years older. The parents were professional middle class, with the usual aspirations to becoming a 'well-constituted' family. So, they were thrilled that their first child was a son and the second a daughter; this they felt was perfection. The boy had a predominant role in the family, not only as a male but also as the elder. He would come to fulfil his parents' academic ambitions for him, while they expected the little girl to continue a familiar, domestic pattern — marry a successful professional and bring up a family of her own. The father was emotionally involved with his daughter, and enjoyed her games and coquettishness; the mother was proud of 'her boy', and showed her affection towards him in an easy and natural way.

Both children felt secure and confident in their respective roles. However, this did not prevent them from quarrelling because of intense sibling rivalry: they each accused the other of being mother's or father's favourite, and often expressed a wish to be the only child in order to get both parents' exclusive attention. This was done with antagonism, but also with warmth since they were very close to each other.

This well-balanced, harmonious, and symmetrical wholeness was abruptly shattered. At the age of fourteen, the boy fell ill and was taken to a medical practitioner who misdiagnosed his illness. Two days later he died in the operating theatre from an acute abdominal infection. The father reacted catastrophically to his psychic pain. He completely reversed his feelings for his daughter, who had suddenly in his eyes become responsible for her brother's death. He seized the eleven-year-old girl, lifted her to face the dead boy inside the coffin, and shrieked: 'Now, you have got what you wanted, to get rid of him and to be alone.' He immediately dropped her there in front of the astonished mourners, who did not know how to react to this dreadful event. The girl experienced intense numbness, followed by tremendous despair and utter loneliness. She had now been deserted by her brother, who had been not only her best friend but also her symmetrical opposite number. She had been robbed of her father's love; instead, she had his hatred. Her previously caring mother now became emotionally absent, such was her intense grief. This prepubescent eleven-year-old girl's whole world, internal and external, had disintegrated in a few hours. She experienced events that were to fundamentally change her own destiny. She found her expectations about herself and her gender completely reversed. The old cliché of the academically successful boy and the domestically content girl was no longer available.

A week later, as she was about to leave for her brother's memorial service, she was struck by abdominal pain, and felt scared when she saw blood coming from her vagina. Nobody was at hand to help her or reassure her about this sudden event. Still, her body had taken care of her, making sure that with her menarche she would be reaffirmed in her own gender. This was a healthy signal that the expectations of others, that she would

MOTHER,
MADONNA,
WHORE

take her brother's place and even replace him, could never be fulfilled. She was now sure of her own gender-identity. But, despite this physiological sign, she remained in need of further reassurance in the face of her own bereavement and the need not to disappoint her parents.

Her father's behaviour became more violent. He could not accept his son's death; he was full of revenge and armed himself with a gun to search for the doctor who had misdiagnosed his son's illness. My patient was very much the target for his pathological mourning. He made her wear black for two years and forced her to accompany him to the cemetery to visit her brother's grave twice a week. The first physical and emotional expressions of her femininity were met with derision and contempt by her father. He was now besieged by jealousy, and any attempts she made at asserting her femininity he answered with rage. He began to beat her regularly, using any pretext he could find to make her feel humiliated and ashamed of being a woman. (In his own way, he was committing a sort of incestuous pattern with her.) He could not stand the thought of her being with a boy, and forbade her to meet anyone outside school hours.

Her mother was still deeply depressed, and remained emotionally detached from all these events. She herself had been a bright, cheerful, pretty girl, with much intellectual potential, but for financial and social reasons she had been unable to pursue an academic career. She had been affected as a young girl by a rheumatic illness, and as a sequel had contracted a heart condition because of which the medical profession had advised her not to pursue any pregnancy because it could have harmful effects on her health. Despite this, she had gone ahead with two pregnancies. After her brother's death my patient developed a caring and nursing attitude towards her mother and secretly hated her father. Just as a son would have done, she dreamt of getting rid of him and taking care of her mother by herself.

At the age of seventeen my patient unexpectedly embarked on a university degree. She wanted to become a medical doctor. This caused much surprise to everyone who knew her, indeed to herself as well, since she had always been thought to be rather

58   unambitious and had never talked of taking up a professional career. She was by now experiencing a tremendous pressure from within herself to belong to both genders and to fulfil expectations associated with both.

From then on, she began to pursue resolutely what was to prove a highly successful academic career. There were inner longings trying to make themselves felt, but she adamantly refused to heed them; they had to do with her own sexuality. Instead she became anorexic and created much trouble by her refusal to eat. Her parents would say, 'The children in Europe are starving because of the war, so you'd better eat.' She thought to herself, 'How can I eat when all those children are dying? I'd better die too just like my brother.'

Then events took another important turn. Her father was now extremely proud of his daughter and of her achievements. However, her mother did not take kindly to her daughter's determination to become a doctor; she saw this as a travesty and, moreover, as the loss of her nurse, 'a far more appropriate profession for a girl'. She felt insufficiently valued as a mother since the girl was not following in her footsteps; she also continued to feel the intense pain that motherhood had brought her. She was full of envy towards her daughter for the newly acquired freedom and independence which she had never been able to have in her own life.

Ten years after her brother's death, when my patient was in her second year at medical school, her mother suffered a cerebral thrombosis, became unconscious, and died after twenty-four hours. My patient had been with her all along. Yet now her father blamed her for her mother's death. She was left alone with her father, still able to pursue her career but leading a spinster's lifestyle. She had acquired by now several hysterical traits and was extremely inhibited and repressed about sexual matters. She suffered from fainting attacks, and was subject to moodiness and irritability, until she decided to enter psychotherapy. She gained much insight from her therapy, and was able to see that the only way for her to have an individual life was to move away from her father.

MOTHER,   My patient had a few close relationships with women of
MADONNA,
WHORE   different ages which afforded her much satisfaction and gave

relationship which she had once had with her mother. In her tentative relationships with men she chose either brutish men who were rather insensitive to her needs, or ineffectual, weak coevals to whom she devoted her time helping them in their own advancement. So she was trying either to placate or to revitalize them, thus re-enacting a relationship with an angry father or a weak, dead brother.

Unsatisfactory as her emotional life may have been, she did not feel that she could consider becoming a mother. This never appeared to her as a real choice. Years went by before she came to see me following the beginning of her involvement with her colleague. It was only when we disentangled her previous history that she was able to look at her longings to become a mother, which had been suppressed ever since she had felt forbidden to achieve motherhood. Indeed, when she wrote to her father telling him about her pregnancy she got an unprecedentedly prompt reply from him 'warning' her that she might 'still have time to do something about it . . . After all, any woman can have children, you are supposed to do more important things in life.' She felt both flattered and under-mined. This duality in her response reflected her male and female identities.

The history of this particular patient illustrates the intricate and complicated nature of gender-identity and its achievement, as well as the vulnerability and brittleness of adolescence disturbed by a traumatic event. The range of relationships and expectations that an individual believes to be contained within herself is really handed down by others (at least three previous generations). Here is a woman who by most criteria could have been assessed as a normal and accomplished person. Her firm determination not to have children could easily have been considered, as in many other cases, to be the result of clear thinking and a conscious choice. However, she had never made a choice of her own. She had always felt at the mercy of her father's desire to turn her into the resurrection of her dead brother for the sake of his own sense of achievement and pride.

This case history exemplifies the special importance of the inner space in adolescence, and of the biological clock when time is running out. These two phenomena come together in a particular way around the time of the menopause. The menopause is an exclusively female predicament, and its importance should be understood as one more reason why it is inappropriate for theories, including theories of perversion, based on clinical observations of men to be automatically transferred to women.

Whereas a man owns the 'freehold' of his reproductive organs a woman has them only on 'leasehold'. Or perhaps it would be more accurate to say, in Raphael-Leff's (1985) words, that in pregnancy the 'owner-occupier' is taking over her body; but when does the woman feel her body to be completely her own? At the age when women lose their reproductive abilities, men remain untouched in theirs (albeit with fewer spermatozoa than in their youth). Lax puts it thus:

Women's increased narcissistic vulnerability due to the ending of their procreativity may also be heightened by the fact that male procreative capacity does not end during middle age. This fact accounts for a significant difference between the sexes during this phase of the life cycle, namely, a man can, or could, start a new family with children but a woman cannot. (1982, p. 159)

I believe that this difference largely accounts for paedophilia being much more prevalent in men than in women. The 'Lolita syndrome' is often experienced by ageing males in search of an 'immortality' which women of the same age, dominated as they are by the biological clock, can no longer achieve. When an ageing man sees an attractive girl, he may not only fantasize about her sexually, but may also see her as the potential young mother of his future child. Why is it, then, that when an ageing woman is in a parallel situation, seeing a young attractive man, everyone — including herself — assumes that she has in mind her own son? Is there a cultural, sociological process which allows such double standards for men and women? Does narcissism vary according to gender? Or does this 'mark of time' affect narcissism differently in males and females?

It may be appropriate to conclude a chapter which

particularly stresses the power of the womb with an account of the traumatic effects that a hysterectomy, the loss of the womb, can have on women. This is symbolized by the posture of women entering and leaving gynaecological and obstetrical wards. Those who are pregnant enter with a pride in their generous convexity; those who emerge after a hysterectomy tend to do so hunched forward, complementing the imagined concavity of their despoiled abdomen. A U-turn has taken place from birth to destruction.

Men, lacking that 'inner space' which is so important to women, often find it hard to understand the significance of a hysterectomy to a woman. It can be more devastating than the menopause because there is an element of agonizing choice. Despite the intense bleeding associated with severe abdominal pain which may make a hysterectomy advisable, it is seldom medically prescribed on account of 'subjective' symptoms. 'The decision is yours', says the gynaecologist. 'Damn it all' is the woman's reaction.

I have seen women who, at a much earlier age than when menopause would be expected, are going through all sorts of hesitations and doubts before involving themselves in hysterectomy. They have been of all ages, heterosexual and homosexual, some already mothers, some not, others too old to be able to get pregnant but yet in serious doubt because of the loss of an organ which is deeply associated with femininity and womanhood. These women experience an excruciating conflict over giving up that wonderful, creative organ, which could or did make possible the birth of children, the beautiful babies of a woman's real or fantasy world.

The mourning process begins before the operation. For mothers there is a feeling of betrayal in abandoning the organ which meant so much to them. For those women who never experienced the joy and pain of childbirth there is a feeling of pain and loss at giving up for all time the idea of conceiving a baby. This mourning can often be associated with memories of abortion, and there are nightmares in which unborn babies suddenly reassert themselves in the woman's mind.

Motherhood is the central theme of this book — motherhood with all its power for good and, occasionally, for

62   perversion. The inner space, the womb and its mental
representations, is unique to women and is crucial to motherhood. To be deprived of the womb is to experience a true loss of
power in a uniquely female way.

MOTHERHOOD AS A PERVERSION

ODD THOUGH IT MAY SOUND, motherhood provides an excellent vehicle for some women to exercise perverse and perverting attitudes towards their offspring, and to retaliate against their own mothers.

Normal child development is generally held to depend predominantly on healthy mothering, in which mothers derive much pleasure from the process of taking care of their babies and helping them to develop into independent and self-assured human beings with their own unique characteristics. (Winnicott (1965) says that babies achieve their 'true self' through 'good enough mothering'.) However, this is more easily said than done, since mothers are also the children of their own mothers with their own plethora of early experiences and traumas. In the words of Chodorow, 'women's mothering is reproduced across generations' (1978, p. 3), and Blum agrees: 'The human mother continues mothering long after the child's abject dependence, into the adult life of the next generation, and the mothering qualities of grandmotherhood' (1980, p. 95).

In psychoanalysis the word 'perversion' is used exclusively in relation to sexuality, but before Freud's time the term was used to denote 'deviations of instinct', as noted by Laplanche and Pontalis, who add that: 'Those authors who accept a plurality of instincts are thus brought to make a very broad category out of perversion and to posit a multitude of forms for it to take: perversions of the "moral sense" (delinquency), of the "social instincts" (prostitution), of the "instinct of nutrition" (bulimia, dypsomania)' (1973, p. 307). It is strange, though, that while the concept of instinct can be seen to stretch as far as nutrition and its abuse in dypsomania, no mention is made of the perversion of the 'maternal instinct' — a term which in the 'normal' sense has been so widely and loosely used. In other words, 'perverse motherhood' has almost never been acknowledged. A rare exception is J. N. Rosen, who eloquently says:

The concept of perversion of the maternal instinct fits every fact I have observed about the aetiology of schizophrenia. It fits the behaviour of the mothers of schizophrenics, it fits the material obtained from psychotic patients, and it fits the biological fact that any instinct, in expressing itself, can become subject to perversion. Going through the gamut of instincts, I cannot think of one that is not subject to this law. I cannot think of one that cannot be bent to conform to the faulty aim–object relationship that we call perversion . . . Poisoning comes from the perverse mother who is not gifted with the divine attunement that makes her understand what her baby is crying for and allows her to return it to a world of omnipotent contentment . . . A child has to grow. If it has a parent suffering from a perverted maternal instinct, the child from the start must build on a weakened psychosexual base. (1953, pp. 100–1)

Rosen is concerned with the aetiology of schizophrenia and the understanding of the infant-adult who has suffered through the effects of the 'perverse mother', whereas I am concerned with the behaviour of the latter.

This chapter deals with the findings on motherhood as a perversion and its many implications. These comments are supported by clinical material.

In trying to explain this process, I shall draw on two separate strands of evidence. Firstly, there are the adult male patients who have not only told of their early childhood experiences with their mothers, but also relive in their transference the kind of engulfment and dependency they have gone through. They try to make the therapist re-enact or dramatize their own past histories. In this connection, we can learn from the work of Mahler (1963) on the 'symbiosis' and 'separation/ individuation' stages in normal infant development, and from Glasser's (1979) work on 'the core complex', in which there is a deep-seated and pervasive longing for an intense and most intimate closeness to another person, amounting to a 'merging', a 'state of oneness', 'a blissful union'. This is never realized, partly because whenever such a person has the opportunity to be emotionally close to another, he experiences a threat to his identity and withdraws (pp. 278–80). This is very much in evidence in the transferential process, in which the patient re-enacts a fantasy of fusion originating with his mother, who allowed him neither individuation nor separation. In my view, this desire for fusion is not a defence against envy, which is the usual Kleinian hypothesis, but, as Hopper (1986) has argued, a defence against aphanisis, or anxieties concerning annihilation and helplessness, which is just as likely to precede or provoke envy as to follow or result from it.

Secondly, there are the perverse female patients who have talked of their relationships with their children and how they abuse their power and control over their offspring. Again and again, the mother's mental health emerges as crucial for the development of her offspring. We learn this lesson for example from Greenson, who describes his work with a transsexual–transvestite five-and-a-half-year-old-boy:

I believe women's certainty about their gender-identity and men's insecurity about theirs are rooted in early identification with the mother . . . The mother may promote or hinder the dis-identifying and the father does the same for the counter-identification . . . The boy must attempt to renounce the pleasure and security-giving closeness that identification with the mother affords, and he must form an identification with the less accessible father . . . The mother must be willing to allow *the boy to identify with the father figure.* (1968, pp. 371 ff., my emphasis)

Greenacre (1960) and Mahler (1968) have pointed out the important part the father plays in helping the child to resolve the symbiosis with the mother. The father of separation and of individuation thereby becomes a facilitator of the separation/individuation process. Loewald sees the role of the father as a positive supporting force for the pre-oedipal child against the threat of re-engulfment by the mother: 'Against this threat of the maternal engulfment, the paternal position is not another threat or danger, but a support of powerful force' (1951, p. 15).

As early as 1968, Rascovsky and Rascovsky in their now classical study on filicide called our attention to the frequent and serious injuries inflicted upon the infant by parental acting-out. These included 'the traumatic vicissitudes of pregnancy and delivery, circumcision, disturbances in natural or artificial lactation, and especially the qualitative and quantitative variations in abandonment'. They regarded these factors as responsible for 'an increase in born hostility and envy and consequently responsible for adult acting out and psychopathic behaviour'. These authors noted that the neglect of this area in the psychoanalytical literature could be regarded as 'an aspect of the universal resistance to acknowledging the *mother's filicide drives, undoubtedly the most dreaded and uncanny truth for us to face*' (1968, p. 390, my italics). In a later paper, the same authors stress the decisive importance of the parental attitude on innate infantile aggressiveness and assert that parricide 'must be regarded as a consequence of filicidal behaviour, and its principal roots must be attributed to the infant's identification with the parents' aggression' (1972, p. 271). They go on to remind us of parents' destructive behaviour towards their children, expressed either through active or passive attitudes such as 'early or repeated abandonment, mental or physical punishment, cruelty, physical or verbal attacks, [and] indifference to suffering' (p. 272). They also add that the affected child introjects these experiences as internal persecutory objects which are very much connected with the actual parents and not just fantasied ones.

Filicide, though, is an ancient practice and it is related partly to the parents' ambivalence. As Blum has remarked: 'the full historical and psychological implications of infanticide and of derivative expressions of child sacrifice in mistreated babies and battered children have probably only been thoroughly studied in this century, the century of the child, and the century of psychoanalysis . . . Psychoanalysis actually began with the study of child abuse prior to the discovery of universal incestuous conflicts in children and their parents.' He argues that 'the child's needs for socialization could be used as a ready target for the discharge of parents' antisocial impulses . . . The omnipotent parent can be assured of victory in power struggles with the child' (1980, pp. 109–10).

According to Benedek, 'Disturbed mothering turns the symbiotic relationship into a vicious circle. This leads to introjection of objects and self-representations in the child charged with aggressive cathexis' (1959, p. 397).

It is amazing how maltreated babies respond in a complementary way to their mother's exploitation: it seems they sense this as a means of survival. They are terrified of losing their mother, and therefore their own existence. The mechanism of splitting as described by Kernberg (1975) is understood by Blum (1980) for this purpose as follows: 'The punitive parent may be defensively idealized or split off from a "good object" image. The "denigrated, bad self" identified with the denigrated punitive parent image is often repressed. Contradictory ego ideals may be maintained in consciousness in a "vertical split" in which full awareness of the inconsistencies is defensively avoided' (Blum, p. 111). After all, the child relies for survival on an 'auxiliary ego' (Spitz, 1946, 1951) initially provided by parents. This has been observed in many studies of the effects of the parent–child relationship (see for example Bowlby, 1951, 1958; Bowlby *et al.*, 1956; Burlingham and Freud, 1943). A similar process has been described by Masterson and Rinsley (1975) in the mother's role in the aetiology of the borderline personality. The authors stress the effects on the baby of the alternation between maternal libidinal availability (reward) and its withdrawal at the time of separation/ individuation. The baby, a future borderline personality, responds to its mother's rewards by the denial of separateness. This, in itself, confirms the child's acting out of his reunion fantasies with that maternal part-object, and promotes his dependency and his fears of being abandoned if he dares to individuate. Similar findings are produced by Lothstein (1979), who stresses the role of the mother in the aetiology of transsexualism in his studies of the mothers of male and female transsexuals. According to him, 'These mothers are unable to tolerate their sons' separation and individuation via masculine identifications and remain attached to their sons via feminine identifications. They seem to perceive the male child's gender separateness as a threat to their own personal integrity.' Lothstein describes a process which operates in the upbringing of daughters who become transsexuals:

These mothers also experience their daughters' prolonged and continued identifications as a threat to their personal integrity. By actively pushing their daughters away from feminine identifications, they seem to be protecting themselves from symbiotic fusion and regression. Our clinical data suggest that their daughters' male identifications may be partially defensive, to ward off both their and their mothers' murderous wishes toward each other. (p. 221)

He then hypothesizes that the mother's 'proneness to disrupt one of her child's gender-identities will vary as a function of the sex of the child, the stresses in her marriage, her current relationship to her own mother, and the current status of her *bisexual* conflict' (p. 222, my italics). These children comply with their mothers' wishes as their only way of survival, and in so doing they create a false sense of self with structural ego defects and ego weaknesses.

In Benedek's words, 'Psychoanalysis often demonstrates that parents become aware of their own unconscious motivations towards their children by anticipating the child's behaviour and its unconscious motivations . . . It seems that parents and children, like paranoids, achieve what they anticipate with anxiety, and intend to avoid' (1959, p. 406).

The woman who struggled through her own childhood with
a punitive mother, in submission to her own superego,
identifies with the aggressive mother and may easily attack the
disappointing and depriving child (Steele, 1970). That child is
experienced by her as not fulfilling her own unconscious
motivations in pursuing motherhood.

Let us examine the raw psychological basis for this process in
familiar, everyday terms. It is generally accepted that we learn
from mistakes, but what is not so easily recognized is that
'mistakes' are unconsciously linked to experiences we have
gone through in early life. Therefore, we could be oblivious to
the significance of words or actions which suddenly and
unexpectedly appear in our lives. These make a strong impact
on us, especially when we become parents. They make us feel
alienated and afraid of losing our mental representations of
ourselves. For instance, people who have gone through painful
and humiliating experiences with their own parents have
secretly promised to themselves never to behave in the same
way. But the unconscious tricks us mercilessly, and without
any warning something will emerge from within ourselves that
we do not recognize as ours, and takes us by surprise. We
believe that it comes from our parents. That awful parental
voice or action we tried so carefully to avoid re-emerges
forcefully in our dealings with our own children, and
immediately we feel a sense of guilt and shame. I believe that
most of us are only too painfully aware of this happening, and
that, the more aware we are, the more we work through it in
order to solve this inner 'intrusion'. Our goal is to become our
own person, our 'true self' which will enable us to let our
children do the same. But for some this is not so easily achieved,
especially if they have been subjected to repeated humiliating
and damaging experiences.

I tend to agree with Grunberger's (1985) idea that the girl is
unavoidably restricted by being born to someone who is not her
'true' sexual object, and that, because she does not receive from
her mother the same kind of cathexis that would be offered to a
son, the girl is more dependent on her love-objects than the boy
is. There are many ways in which a woman may become
perverse, but in this chapter I shall explore only those

concerning motherhood and a woman's reactions to and acknowledgement of the sex of her own child. Sometimes women are required to make heroic efforts to do the 'right thing', considering what they themselves may have had to go through, especially when they have never felt accepted in their own gender-identity, and the same has happened to their mothers. The process then becomes self-repeating, putting each generation at risk.

A fifty-year-old woman came for treatment because of her proneness to get engaged in extreme sadomasochistic relationships with men. She had been married twice and had had many love-affairs, all of which eventually led to her lover beating her up. She was a bright, intelligent, accomplished woman, a successful professional in the arts. In her first interview she complained bitterly about her mother, who she still regarded as a 'bloody cow', and who, she claimed, had instilled in her a submissive and subdued attitude towards men. This, she believed, had to do with the fact that when she was four her brother was born, and she was then sent to boarding school. She had been made to feel a nuisance all her life, and her mother was barely able to tolerate her.

She had been her father's favourite, but this completely ceased with the arrival of the baby boy. She then felt deserted and without any affection from either parent. Her mother went overboard about her son and encouraged a bickering relationship between the two siblings, which aroused in my patient intense rivalry and hatred towards men. She was able, though, to sublimate these feelings in her professional career, where she felt 'as good or even better than a man'. However, she always chose weak and ineffectual men as partners, which reinforced her conviction of being better than them. She became very critical of them, to the point of denigrating them in a ferocious way, which led them to abuse her physically.

She had two children from her first marriage. She found her own history repeated when she had first a girl and then, four years later, a boy. Despite her intelligence and insight into her own situation she was unable to prevent herself from falling

into the same pattern as her mother: there she was, trying to treat her children with equal devotion, but not succeeding. She felt a tremendous rivalry with her daughter from the moment she was born, and was unable to handle the strong hostility she felt towards her. This was not easy to acknowledge then, but much later on, when her daughter became a beautiful young adolescent, she found herself behaving exactly as her own mother had to her.

Although she wanted to get rid of her daughter she nevertheless persisted in her wish to be a good mother. Yet she was blind to the problems her daughter was experiencing. The girl had associated with a criminal, and when on one occasion she came home covered with bruises it transpired that this man was using the young girl for prostitution and for drug-dealing. Meanwhile, the son had some notable academic achievements to his credit, but was unable to make any associations within his peer group, such was the close bond he had established with his mother. During treatment my patient arrived at many deep and painful realizations about herself and the perverse ways in which she had redirected her intense hatred towards her mother in her dealings with her own children. She had failed to give her daughter any reassurance about or support for her femininity; female self-denigration had taken hold in the third successive generation. Her daughter did not feel deserving of a good relationship with a coeval and had engaged in sadomasochistic relationships, just like her mother. As for her son, she had never allowed any process of individuation to occur.

Greenacre (1968) says that in her experience of dealing with sexually perverse patients there seems to have been a definite disturbance of development in the first two years of life. This affects and undermines the orderly progression of the work of separation and individuation.

A failure of satisfactory maternal care, the mother either depriving or overwhelming the infant, makes a fertile ground for the later development of perverse tendencies, but this failure by itself does not offer conditions for the specific perverse content. It means that there is a prolongation of the uncertainty about the 'I' and the 'Other', and there already exists a situation conducive to continued oscillation in relationships. These conditions also tend to make for an

MOTHERHOOD
AS A
PERVERSION

impairment or slowing of object-relationship, and consequently for a greater retention of primary aggression, and an increase in secondary aggression by frustration . . . This is later transformed into sadism as a response to the mother's assault. (1968, pp. 53–4)

My clinical observations show that mothers who display perverse tendencies towards their offspring do so within the first two years of their children's life. In Winnicott's (1953) terms, the 'transitional object' is used by the pervert to be invented, manipulated, used and abused, ravaged and discarded, cherished and idealized, symbiotically identified with and deanimated all at once. This is exactly what I believe takes place in the perverse mother's mind and through her manipulations of her baby. In other words, the baby becomes for such a mother her 'transitional object', as proposed by Stoller (1968). Granoff and Perrier (1980) make a similar comment on the type of perverse relationship a mother establishes with her baby in which the baby is first identified as her missing phallus, and then becomes her 'toy' or 'thing'; this they see 'as analogous to the "part-object" relationships of fetishistic perverts' (p. 85, my translation).

As I have said, as a clinician I have observed that the main difference between male and female perverse action lies in the aim. Whereas in men the act is aimed at an external part-object, in women it is against themselves: either against their bodies or against objects of their own creation — that is, their babies. In both respects, bodies and babies are treated as part-objects. In this context I remember a patient who was referred for psychiatric assessment because of violent behaviour directed towards her second child. Her first pregnancy had come as a surprise to her, but she decided to go ahead with it, regarding it as taking out insurance against a dread of being alone. The child could become utterly dependent on her and totally under her control. When this first baby arrived, she was overcome by feelings of repulsion and revulsion against it. She felt ready to kick it, and after reflection she decided that in order to overcome these feelings she would fix in her mind the idea of the baby being part of herself; on some days she would choose her right arm to be the baby, on others it would be one of her legs. In this way she felt able to master her impulses to beat up her first child. Later, with her second baby she asserted, 'There is no more room in my body for a second one. All has been used up by the first one.'

She was a careerist thief who had spent more than ten years in different prisons. From childhood she compulsively stole money, clothes, jewellery — in fact anything from anybody. She managed in this early period never to get caught, but nevertheless was sent to detention centres because she was unmanageable and her parents were unable to cope with her. Later on she specialized in stealing from smart department stores, and also developed a technique for housebreaking. She did most of the stealing on her own since she did not trust anyone. She said that, had she used her money correctly, she would now be rich but that 'part of the thieves' personality was to grab and then spend too freely'. She described graphically her feelings when tempted in a store. At no time did she think of her victims, neither did she show guilt or shame. She stood before an object trying to convince herself how awful it would be if she were caught and particularly awful for her pets (she never mentioned her children in this regard), who would suffer if she went to prison; in the end she sometimes stole 'a treat for them as well'. Sometimes she could pay for the goods in front of her but she said to herself: 'You would be silly to eat up capital.' All this is not to say that she did not experience much suffering from the consequences of her actions and she was miserable at the prospect of more imprisonment, such was her degree of ambivalence.

When I first saw her she told me that her first child, a boy, had given her for the first time 'a sense of consciousness'. She went on to describe what she meant by saying that before she became a mother she was completely unaware that her actions would affect any other human being. She found this discovery unbearable because she would hear her boy's voice inside her head when she was in prison, and she knew that the boy needed his mother. With a very conscious determination she decided that the only way to cope successfully with this situation would be to stop thinking of him in terms of somebody outside her, and to believe instead that he was part of her body, so that they became only one person: 'both my baby and myself were in a cocoon'. When the boy was three, a girl was born but she could not bring herself to include the girl in this cocoon. She found all the girl's demands excessive, became violent towards her, and began to batter her. She hated the girl for a long time and saw her only as an intruder in her life. She then admitted how much vengeful satisfaction she had derived from her compulsive beating of her daughter, although she felt sick about these actions afterwards.

Another patient sought treatment because of her intense and compulsive need for physical affection from her daughter, aged seven. After three years of treatment, when she could look at her basic distrust towards her therapist and an intense fear of being swamped in the transferential process, she described how her daughter had 'diagnosed' her disturbance accurately by saying, 'Mum, I think that when you decided to have me you wanted a baby and you never thought that the baby would grow up. Now I'm ten you still treat me like a baby and you won't let me go.' By then, she had come to terms with her vicarious source of sensual gratification from her small baby and her intense anger at her growing up and becoming independent.

A further patient came to consult me, feeling distraught and confused. She had a baby of two years with whom she felt unable to cope, and whenever she felt frustrated or annoyed she would beat up her baby. This would relieve her of her anxiety and she would use it for sexual gratification. Suddenly she stopped these beatings altogether when she realized that her baby had a triumphant look and, according to her, 'he was even enjoying' her ill treatment of him. She became aware at this point that the baby had the upper hand since he felt able to manipulate her into losing her temper. He had now become 'the master'.

According to Stoller, 'The hostility in perversion takes form in a fantasy of revenge hidden in the actions that make up the perversion and serves to convert childhood trauma into adult triumph' (1975, p. 4). In my clinical experience, the opportunity that motherhood offers of being in complete control of a situation creates fertile ground for some women who have experienced injurious and traumatic events in their own lives to exploit and abuse their babies. Thus are produced mothers of battered babies, of transsexuals, and — above all — of male sexual perverts.

It is often the male sexual pervert's early relationship with his mother which is the most influential determinant of his distorted object-relationships in later life. We accept that mothers of battered babies are insecure and emotionally deprived people. In their accounts of how beatings take place, there is an element of triumph over the raging baby. The same pattern is seen with mothers who clothe their boy babies as girls, or vice versa; revenge is always there, as well as a threat of withdrawal of the mother's love unless the boy behaves like a girl. These mothers have not been able to acknowledge their child's gender and have exploited their controlling power to assign it a different gender. It is no coincidence that as babies they themselves went through experiences humiliating to their womanhood. There is not only the element of revenge, but also some dehumanization of the object. As McDougall says,

The early mother-image plays a continuing, essential role in the unconscious of all neosexual creators. The idealized maternal image not only suggests that the mother is devoid of sexual desire but also contains an implicit denial of the importance of genital differences. The belief that the differences between the sexes plays no role in the arousal of sexual desire underlies every neosexual scenario. (1986, p. 249)

We have learnt from Stoller (1968) that one of the very important components in the production of the child's core gender-identity is the infant–parent relationship, in particular the psychological aspects of the oedipal and pre-oedipal relationships. The mother's acknowledgement of her child's sex plays an extremely important part in establishing and confirming its core gender-identity.

I shall attempt to illustrate the significance of motherhood in the production of the child's core gender-identity by some clinical material about another patient, this time a male, in his mid-forties and married with four children, who referred himself by letter. Let him explain his own predicament:

I have lived with a condition for most of my life which manifests itself in the form of transvestial or transsexual behaviour and feelings. Whilst I am able to suppress these feelings for a good deal of the time, there nevertheless comes a moment when I can cope no longer – as has happened now . . . and for the first time self-mutilation seems to be logical . . . I desperately need someone to help me decide upon the best way to contain or suppress it, or to suggest some way in which I could free myself of my now unremitting torment . . . The symptoms that I am experiencing at the moment fall into two quite distinct categories, i.e. mental and physical. Mentally, I feel that I am a woman in the cliché situation of having to masquerade my way through life simply because I am not as perfect as I want to be . . . I can quite see the clear possibilities of a 'change'. To this end I have now almost cut myself off emotionally from those around me – and so the conflict rages, as I question: to whom does my first loyalty lie, my family, all of whom are and will be able to make lives of their own, or to myself, with one precious life only? . . . On the physical side, the tension can only be relieved by wearing anything other than men's clothes . . . More obvious symptoms, physical side that is, are: morning sickness, vomiting through the day, loss of appetite, feeling shivery, aching in the small of the back and the most obvious sign that tells me when I am about to 'go under' again – that my breasts become tender and sore – and it is at these times that the sensation of my nipples touching against my woolly jumper makes me just want to scream . . .

And so on. From his own description of his problem, we can vividly experience his enormous despair and sense of despondency and desolation.

There is not much happiness or fulfilment where perversions are concerned, as this case clearly demonstrates. Let us now briefly explore the patient's early background. As might well be expected, it is most complicated and peculiar. He was surrounded by all sorts of perverting attitudes throughout his

MOTHER,
MADONNA,
WHORE

early life. He was the younger child in a family of two, with an older sister. When he was one year old (during the war) he was sent to stay with one of his aunts for 'reasons of safety'. His early recollections had to do with feelings of being lost. He remembered his time with his aunt as an extremely confused one. She was a warm and kind woman, but suddenly at the age of three she made it very clear to him that unless he complied with all her wishes, she would withdraw her love. The conditions she imposed included not only wearing girl's clothes, but behaving like one. He still remembers with trepidation that period of his life. At the beginning he tried to go against his aunt's whims, but soon he realized that the consequence could be complete isolation. After all, he had already been given away by his own mother, from whom he received a few postcards but never a visit. He then started to comply with everything required of him.

The aunt had had a daughter, who died at a very early age. She now decided to send her nephew to an all-girls school and taught him how to behave like a girl; for medical visits she would come to London and have him examined by a doctor friend of hers. At the age of twelve, he convincingly looked like a girl. On the occasion of a family member's wedding, he was made the bridesmaid. He became the object of the most extraordinary scandal when, during the ceremony, his real mother — who had not seen him since she had sent him to live with his aunt — suddenly realized that this beautiful 'girl' who was accompanied by 'her' aunt was in fact her son. Amid screams, cries, and shouts he was taken away by his real mother, who not only severely punished him but proceeded immediately to send him to an all-boys school. There, his suffering, torment, and humiliation became so great that eventually his mother decided to send him back to his aunt, pronouncing him too sissy and stupid for her to be concerned with him any further. He was glad to return to his aunt, but things were never to be as they had been before. He now had to suffer his aunt's denigration for his 'maleness'. I prefer not to go any further into this case here; what has been said is sufficient to convey the horrors the two women in their role of mother together inflicted on this poor boy from infancy to adolescence.

MOTHERHOOD
AS A
PERVERSION

There are few psychoanalytical studies dealing with the particular psychopathology of perverse relations between mother and child. However, among them Sperling's (1959, 1964) are helpful in providing further understanding of the findings I am putting forward. The following quotations are from these papers: 'It is difficult to assess correctly the aetiological value of certain childhood experiences on the lives of perverts from reconstructions of their analysis, especially if striking differences of seduction are absent' (1959, p. 236); '. . . in my opinion, deviate sexual behaviour in children is dynamically a disturbance of the superego resulting from the internalization of certain unconscious parental attitudes. I consider it an essential therapeutic requirement in the case of children to modify the unconscious attitudes of the objects from whom this superego is derived' (1959, p. 238). 'I have found that the relationship between mother and child, which I have described [1959] as *the perverse type of object-relationship*, was a genetic factor in the pathological ego and superego functioning of the child' (1964, p. 484, my italics).

Nevertheless, it is disappointing that even though Sperling refers to a '*perverse type of object-relationship*', and takes mothers of transvestite boys in analysis prior to taking the children, she never again refers to perverse motherhood. An exception may be when she talks in a casual manner of the two mothers involved, and says: 'Both mothers functioned adequately sexually and enjoyed being women. The role of a woman was not deprecated: in fact, certain feminine activities, *especially maternal functions*, were highly valued. In comparison, the role of the man appeared to be less important in some respects because he was not trusted with the care of the children' (1964, p. 485, my italics). Even when Sperling is advocating the treatment of mothers of perverse children, she fails to conceptualize any perverse attitudes in their motherhood, and refers instead to 'maternal functions [which] were highly valued'. For my part, I believe that those patients were abusing their position of power as mothers, and that they were exhibiting what I would call perverse maternal attitudes. As I have said in Chapter 1, the failure to diagnose these women correctly results partly from society's glorification of

motherhood and its refusal even to consider that it may have a
dark side.

Gallwey says:

*Women have an advantage over men here by being more able to
use their bodies directly, together with socially based
encouragements to corporal idealization,* to support the
fantasy of actually being the early nurturing objects in idealized
form . . . *This is probably one reason why sexual perversions,
most forms of criminal behaviour, and a general overreliance
on domineering modes of conduct are so much more common
in men who have further to go in sustaining their conviction of
successfully identifying with or dominating prototypic ideal
maternal objects.* (1985, p. 134, my emphasis)

In this excellent work Gallwey gets very close to the essence
of perverse female sexuality in motherhood where the
'nurturing object' can become, under stressful conditions, an
object of absolute dominance and control, but he veers away
from this conclusion because of his over-idealization of the
female body and of motherhood. He dismisses the mother's
potential perverting capacities.

The importance of unconscious motivations to become a
mother should not be overlooked. The research by Raphael-
Leff (1983) on the models of mothering and on the impact the
baby has on the mother is relevant. She describes two basic
models of mothering. One is the 'regulator', in which the
mother expects the baby to adapt to herself; the other is the
'facilitator', in which the mother adapts to the baby. This
study was carried out on professional middle-class women.
Raphael-Leff is concerned with the effects (pact-impact) the
baby has on its mother's 'hopes and promises'. It seems to me
that in women with severe psychopathology the facilitator
mother who welcomes the infant's intense dependence on her
and the exclusive intimacy of their symbiosis is prone, when
severely disturbed, to bring up transvestite, fetishistic, or
transsexual boys. On the other hand, the regulator mother
could be more prone, again in extreme cases, to be the mother
of battered babies.

Rinsley (1978) offers us similar findings in describing the mother–infant interaction in the genesis of borderline psycho-pathology. Here, the mother rewards the baby for passiveness and dependency, and withdraws her affection when confronted with its aggression or assertiveness. According to Rinsley, the mother of the future borderline adolescent and adult enjoys her infant's abject dependency, and consistently thwarts its innate drive towards separation/ individuation. This enjoyment in its pure form is short-lived, lasting only from birth to the second postnatal month. Thus, says Rinsley,

Typically the borderline mother, embarked upon raising a future borderline child and adult, smilingly exuded happy satisfaction when asked about her experiences with her neonate, only to lapse into frowning, emotional blandness or disdain when discussing her progressively more active infant during the latter half of the first postnatal year and beyond... The mother of the future borderline individual deals with him essentially as she was herself dealt with during this critical period by her own mother.... There was no joy in motherhood for the psychotic mother, who could only respond to her infants by depersonifying them into transitional or fetish-like objects. (pp. 45–6)

Some women also have perverse attitudes towards functions related to motherhood, during which the baby's body has long occupied their own. We have already seen that a woman may have perverse unconscious motivations when she gets pregnant, and is perversely manipulating her own body. At delivery she feels labour pains in her body which can be very severe. Some women feel a great need to 'cling' to their babies' bodies and possess them totally; birth constitutes a challenge to that primary need. The mother experiences a sense of outrage, even a desire for revenge, when the baby is alive and in some ways independent. She now not only sees herself with an impover-ished body, but also feels deeply humiliated by that crucial separation. This is experienced as a total blow. The new being is now struggling to conquer a space of its own. The shock is extreme. After all, the pregnant woman is immediately recognized as such, and society awards her all relevant privileges, cares, and benefits, only to withdraw them abruptly the moment she has the baby. Worse, she is now the sole recipient of all its new emotional, physiological, and biological demands. This could partly explain postnatal depression.

Here again, we note the important part that the mother's emotional sense of equilibrium plays. It is basic to the infant's ability to separate and individuate from its mother, as well as to assume its own gender-identity. The mother of the future pervert does exactly the opposite. Like Sperling before her, Chasseguet-Smirgel (1985b) describes the process of the relationship between mother and son and how the mother interferes with her son's development, but she does not explicitly ascribe this to any perverse maternal attitude. The mother is considered only in terms of her status as the mother of a pervert — obviously a boy. She goes further, saying: 'A feature of the aetiology of the perversions that has often been noted is the very frequent occurrence of an attitude of seduction and complicity on the part of the mother towards her child' (p. 12). There is no description of the mother's psychopathological features, even though it is she who has promoted the perverse development of her child's personality.

I suggest that motherhood is sometimes chosen for unconscious perverse reasons. The woman would know that in achieving motherhood she is automatically achieving the role of master, in complete control of another being who has to submit himself or herself not only emotionally, but also biologically to the mother's demands, however inappropriate they may be. Indeed, as is generally accepted, some women who feel inadequate and insecure find a child becomes the only available source of emotional nourishment, and a craving for physical affection is unloaded on the child. The mothers I have worked with sometimes worry about the adverse effects this could have on the child, but at other times they appear to be unconcerned.

Parents are sometimes unable to respond in an adequate way to 'normal' demands because they have gone through humiliating situations related to their own sense of womanhood or manhood. As we know from Stoller's work, the boy in becoming a man could react to these experiences by producing a perverse psychic structure. According to Chasseguet-Smirgel (1985a), in the boy the perverse structure is established when he is being made to feel, by his mother, that he is her 'perfect partner with his prepubescent penis' (p. 29). But what of the little girl who has been treated by her parents with the utmost contempt from the moment of her birth, merely because she belongs to the female sex? The traditional perverse male solution is not so easily available for her. When she becomes a mother, though, she has other, albeit unconscious ways in which to revenge herself against the fact of being a woman. I am doubtful about Chasseguet-Smirgel's (1985a) idea that perversion is less common in women than in men because a woman has a waiting time for her father as the love-object. It seems to me that the perverse woman is waiting, not so much for her father's love, but for revenge against the denigration she had encountered much earlier on.

Zilbach (1987) fortuitously provides backing for my theory of perverse motherhood when, as described above, she defines her own concept of female 'active engulfment' as part of normal female development. I suggest that a perverse mother makes use of and twists this 'active engulfment' in such a way that she experiences her baby as part of herself, never to let it go or develop its own gender-identity, let alone individuate. She derives a great sense of elation in making her baby respond to her own inappropriate needs.

We can see some of the psychodynamic principles which operate in perversions appearing in females when they become mothers. Woman's capacity for procreation — that is, getting pregnant and containing the baby within her own body — provides her with some of the same emotional characteristics in her object-relationships as are found in exaggerated and highly distorted forms in perverse relationships. These include the desires to engulf the other person, to dehumanize the object, and to invade, take complete control of, and merge with the Other.

Isn't it amazing that while Oedipus, Coriolanus, and Hamlet are frequently and fully analysed, little attention has been paid to Jocasta, Volumnia, and Gertrude? These are

among the best-known literary examples of deviant motherhood, mothers who exploit and abuse the power they have over
their sons. So far the literature (with a few exceptions, notable
among them Stewart's (1961) 'Jocasta's crimes') has been
exclusively occupied with understanding the psychopathology
of the sons.

Another instance from literature is Medea, who exemplifies
not only the power of motherhood, but also how the
'biological clock' determines a woman's actions. Medea is
highly intelligent, in power, loved and in love. When abruptly
and unexpectedly dispossessed of all this, she becomes aware of
the only power left to her: her children, who become the targets
for her revenge against their father, Jason. When he decides to
abandon her for a much younger and more powerful bride,
Medea skilfully and subtly hatches a plan designed to give as
much pain as possible to Jason — to kill their children. She
feels justified in her actions, such is her agony at her own
predicament, and manages to complete the terrible deed within
the space of twenty-four hours.

My argument is that motherhood as a perversion occurs as a
breakdown of inner mental structures, whereby the mother
feels not only emotionally crippled in dealing with the huge
psychological and physical demands from her baby, but also
impotent and unable to obtain gratification from other
sources. She sees the world around her as non-existent in any
helping, supporting way. It is then that she falls back on
inappropriate and perverse behaviour; this, in turn, makes
her feel powerless. Simultaneously, and paradoxically, she
experiences her perverse behaviour as the only power available
to her through her exclusive emotional and physical authority
over her baby. Hence perverse motherhood must be seen as the
product of emotional instability and inadequate individuation
brought about by a process that spans at least three generations.
But part of the problem lies with society. Our whole culture
supports the idea that mothers have complete dominion over
their babies; thus we encourage the very ideas the perverse
mother exploits. We help neither her nor her children, nor
society in general, if we glorify motherhood so blindly as to
exclude the fact that some mothers can act perversely. In the

84 next chapter I look at specific examples of this, and conclude with a further comment on society's expectations of and attitudes to the position of women.

MOTHER,
MADONNA,
WHORE

D O MOTHERS commit incest more frequently than we think, and more at the mother's initiative than we imagine? Are we blocked from perceiving this by our idealization of motherhood? Surely we are, and this is why even in the original oedipal situation we fail to notice Jocasta's responsibility. Hers is the most important case of incest.

We have always blamed Oedipus rather than his mother. Here we are once more attaching the sole responsibility to the male child, and consequently developing a whole new concept of a complex, taking it for granted that Oedipus unconsciously 'knew' his mother and was behaving perversely by marrying her. In fact Jocasta was far better equipped, even consciously, to recognize Oedipus as her son than vice versa. She was the only one who knew that Oedipus could be alive; Laius believed him dead. Why do we not hold her largely, if not entirely responsible for the enactment of her own incestuous desires? It is clear that, if not perverse herself, she had associated with a most perverse individual: her husband Laius, who was not only homosexual but also paedophiliac — his most important reason for not wanting children. She not only married him, already showing signs of being the willing victim of a perverse partnership (the clinical analogy still applies), but contrived to get him drunk in order to get herself impregnated. In other words, she was already exercising her own power over her offspring, which was to lead her to give him away at birth. She might unconsciously have known that she — or indeed he, the offspring — could pursue the lost relationship, the power of motherhood later being replaced by that of incest, which would be more rewarding for her.

It seems unnecessary for researchers to have developed an Electra complex to parallel the Oedipus complex when Jocasta already fulfils that role. Is this again an obstinate tendency to see women as the weak sex, always the victims and never the perpetrators of sexual assault? Women have always been held to be incapable of effecting their own perverse sexual designs, and young boys reckoned to be the only ones to enact sexual fantasies. I believe that many theories of female sexual development are ill-founded, partly through their being based on a need for an ever-present 'earth-mother', a woman who has been so idealized or perhaps even idolized that her faults are overlooked. She is portrayed as powerless in the penis-envy dilemma or, according to the new feminists, the victim of social attitudes, even perhaps contemptible because she seems of less importance than the male. It looks as though we have all become silent conspirators in a system which, from whatever angle we look at them, women are either dispossessed of all power or made the sexual objects and victims of their male counterparts. We do not accord them any sense of responsibility for their own unique functions, deeply related to fecundity and motherhood, and liable at times to manifest themselves perversely. Why should Jocasta, when both she and Oedipus learn the facts of their incestuous relationship, be the one to promptly commit suicide? Apparently Oedipus cannot immediately grasp what has been happening; the truth must therefore have been much closer to Jocasta's consciousness.

MOTHER,
MADONNA,
WHORE

I was professionally consulted abroad some time ago by a woman who knew about my concern for women in distress. I believe that she talked to me because she could no longer bear extra assurance about confidentiality.

She was a young-looking thirty-eight, smart and neat in her appearance, and able to communicate — though with reluctance and much pain — about her predicament. She remarked that my being a woman made it possible for her to reveal a terrible secret she had been living with for many years. Perhaps, she added, I might understand or at least respond in some empathetic manner.

At first it was difficult to assess clearly why she was so concerned. She talked in alarming terms about her son aged twenty-one and his determination to leave home. What had seemed to be a genuine interest for her son's welfare, was later revealed as an intense despair about herself being left all alone; she saw this literally as the end of her life.

She told me of her personal history.

I was brought up in heaven, nothing was denied to me. Both my parents doted on me. However, when I was seven my father suddenly died, and my mother withdrew from the world and made me the exclusive object of her dedication and devotion. Whereas initially I felt very privileged, later I became aware of an intense suffocation and was impeded in my normal developement. I was not allowed to go to school or to have any friends. I wanted to fight against this invasion of my life, but to no avail. My mother was the constant witness of all my actions. I almost felt she interfered in my thoughts and dreams. If I spent too long in the bathroom, she would come and look at me in strange ways always asking me all sorts of private questions. I believe that she wanted to get inside my head, such was the degree of her intrusion into me. This became much worse when I reached adolescence and I had my first menstrual period. At the beginning she withdrew in horror, as if I had become a disgusting alien, but later she began to warn me in threatening ways of the dangers attached to strange men and about their exclusive and dirty interest in sex. My mother could barely stand my becoming a young woman. In our only outings, to Mass on Sundays, she would be like a wild beast, watching anyone approaching me. She was herself an attractive woman, but extremely stern and strict in her religious upbringing. Nobody was allowed to visit us at home, and we never went anywhere except on the occasion of religious festivals when some relatives used to invite us to their homes. On one of these occasions I met a nice-looking young man who was kind to me, and I fell for him – or perhaps for a way out. I married him at sixteen and got pregnant.

My mother never forgave me for leaving her alone; not even the baby's birth changed her mind. When my son was five my husband was sudenly killed in an accident. My mother came back to me as if I had never left her, but I told her that it would be better if we kept apart. I soon realized that I didn't want my mother with me because I wanted my son for myself, alone without any competition. I created an idyllic relationship with my son to the point that I didn't need any other man in my life.

We went together on holidays. I remember very vividly once at the seaside when miniskirts were fashionable. This was a turning point in my life. My son was then fourteen. I went dancing in the local hotel with some youngsters, and had quite a lot to drink. On my return to our room I saw my son sobbing between the sheets. I was worried and asked him why he was upset. He said that he had watched me dancing and had felt deserted and very jealous of the young men. When he made this statement I experienced an immediate sense of inner peace and great contentment; all previous sufferings and upheavals now seemed futile. I had won: he was all mine. We were together for ever, alone. It just seemed natural for me to get into bed with him and to console him. But I wanted to show him my love in a more natural way. I was high, elated and felt randy. I initiated him in the art of making love. Over a period of time I taught him step by step what to do and how to do it. I created the most wonderful lover and both of us were in ecstasy. This has lasted all these years. Neither of us needed anyone else around. Our world was perfect. He seemed to me to be a happy and relaxed young man.

I took all sorts of precautions to make it appear to the world that we had the normal relationship of mother and son. All my life has been invested in him; I have enough economic security for the situation to last for ever. I never thought that he could betray me. But after leaving high school he began to show signs of restlessness and self-assertion. First, he wanted to go abroad to further his studies, but I could not let him go. To start with it was easy for me to persuade him to stay, but he is still unmoving in his decision to go away from me. My only other association is with my mother, whom I see every Sunday, and even then I feel so brittle about him taking advantage of my being away and seeing someone else. I take care of myself to make myself look younger; I have always done so. Our days and nights are so very rich.

At fifteen he began to write poetry which showed so much passion and maturity that I felt afraid of his teachers reading it and somehow guessing what was going on. He used to recite it to me, but lately he has refused to show it to me. I've examined his papers and discovered that his poetry is now full of desire for revenge, sarcastic and bitter. He has even hatched a very elaborate plot by which he can get rid of me. I don't care if he does. As I have told him, if he leaves me I'll take my life. Anyway, life seems unnecessary without him.

It took me quite a while to regain some sort of neutrality, such was the mixture of strong and confused feelings that this woman's account had aroused in me. I tried to figure out how to respond to her intense pain, desolation, and helplessness. I began to see her at the age of seven, soon after her father's sudden death, and to imagine how this little girl might have felt overwhelmed by conflicting emotions, perhaps at first experiencing extreme shock and numbness, possibly replaced later by elation at being the object of her mother's total attention. Her mother obviously went into a pathological mourning in which denial and isolation were used extensively. The little girl was never allowed to mourn her father openly, for she did not want to upset mother. By then, she was so enjoying being her mother's only object of constant care that she might have felt rather guilty about her father's death. The two of them created a closed circle which was broken when the girl began to approach puberty, for it was then that her mother felt threatened in her close association with her daughter, who in turn began to feel the suffocating quality of this relationship (which might even have had incestuous overtones). It is possible that my patient began to harbour murderous designs against her mother and considered that the only solution was to flee from her in a manic heterosexual gesture through her premature marriage.

She might have had sexual problems with her husband, and felt resentful about being cut off from her mother and loaded with the many responsibilities of her own motherhood. It was then that she was faced with yet another unexpected death, which left her in a parallel situation to that of her mother during her childhood. However, this time she was in the controlling position. Like her mother she was unable to work through her bereavement, but resorted to the familiar, manic response with her own child, of creating a perfect circle. Could she escape the destiny of doing to her son whatever had been done to herself? Could she allow herself to give him some sense of individuation, to let him grow up and lead a life of his own? Or would she use the situation in a more skilful way than her mother had, giving the boy so much gratification that it would be difficult, almost impossible even, for him to leave her? She had two alternatives, or let us say she could see only two options: to try to get back to her mother, or to secure her son as her future partner. She didn't need much time to decide upon the latter course. I had to remind myself that this woman, because of her own history and her lack of available resources outside and inside herself, felt unable to see any other solution. She was caught up; she felt she had no alternative. Was she a perverse mother, because she used her son as her sexual partner? I believe that she was a perverse sufferer. Having been a victim, she had later become a victimizer, using her position of dominance to secure her son as her exclusive source of sexual gratification.

I felt much compassion for this patient and for her predicament in a three-generational process, and recalled an insight of Shengold's: 'I have found supervisees to be, in general, more aware of the countertransference tendency to *blame* parents than the tendency to *spare* them. The therapist's need (despite intellectual acceptance) to deny when parental destructiveness appears is as intense and as complex as the similarly held need to deny the Oedipus complex' (1979, p. 554, author's italics). But ever since I have been asking myself how I would have reacted had I been a man. I have to recognize that my initial confused reaction might have been due to my own masculine component feeling outraged. But if I had been a man would my reaction have been stronger? Would I perhaps have identified with the son, full of rage because of this woman's outrageous behaviour?

This leads me to the countertransference phenomenon encountered in the course of my daily professional work: how our gender leads us to respond to our patients' explicit psychopathology. Patients who suffer from gender-dysphoria problems often have strong feelings about, as they say, 'the sex' of the diagnostician or therapist. I have also found that recorded accounts of the same patient differ according to the diagnostician's gender. This difference of response is certainly the outcome not only of patients' transference, but also of our own way of reacting to and interpreting their predicaments. Ganzarain and Buchele (1986) recount their experiences as co-therapists with a group of adults having a history of incest. They provide us with courageous and illuminating comments about their countertransference to these patients in which many feelings are apparent, including disbelief, excited curiosity, sexual fantasies, and desire to rescue. In their own work they were able to talk to one another as female and male therapist about how different interventions with patients had made them feel in their own gender. They also point out that there is virtually nothing in the psychoanalytical literature dealing with this subject.

Needless to say, neither gender has the correct answer or is better equipped than the other to deal with those involved in incest, abusers or abused; but we have a duty to acknowledge our own different responses when assessing or treating them. This might also help us to understand society's different responses to the problems posed by our male and female patients involved in sexual abuse.

I found very refreshing Shengold's discussion of why mother–son incest happens much less frequently than between father and daughter. He asks: 'Is it because most psychiatrists are male and have a deep resistance to the uncovering or the publication of the fulfilment of the male's characteristic forbidden oedipal wish?' (1980, p. 462). He candidly admits to his struggle in thinking about the problem, while writing this paper to overcome his own resistance to the power of this idea.

In the same paper, he describes his patient as a man who came for treatment in his thirties because he was depressed and unhappy. He had been subjected to an incestuous relationship with his mother when he was a precocious adolescent. He was the first child; his mother had had a strong wish for a girl, and forced him to wear a girl's costume and to look like a girl, but to behave like a boy. She was obsessed with ministrations to his body, then forgot about him until he became twelve, when she began to be intensely curious in him and to behave intrusively towards him. Eventually, they started an incestuous relationship which lasted for a few weeks. This was characterized by the mother seducing her son and achieving orgasms from the encounters, while the son was unable to reach ejaculation. This state of affairs was never mentioned or acknowledged; it ended abruptly when the boy had his first ejaculation during sexual intercourse with his mother. At this point she shrieked, became violently disturbed, and rushed away. The incest was never to be repeated or even mentioned. Shengold offers the following explanation: 'In retrospect I feel that my patient, like his mother, and in identification with his mother, was unable to face the implications of the possibility of impregnating her' (1980, p. 471). He clearly sees the mother as the seducer and describes how the son took much of the responsibility for the incest and for the parental guilt, blaming himself more than his mother. Shengold further says that 'in mother–son incest the mother is directly involved in the deed, and is *central* to the fantasies of both son and mother' (p. 470, my italics). So, again, it is disappointing that he fails to recognize or to speculate about the mother's perverse psychopathology, even though he accurately questions the usual diagnosis of such mothers as psychotics and refuses to label his patient's mother as such.

For my own part, I believe that this mother was exhibiting

from early on perverting attitudes towards her son. She appears to me very much the mother of the future pervert described by Chasseguet-Smirgel (1985a) who finds her pre-oedipal son with his prepubescent penis her ideal partner. It seems clear to me that it was not the son's decision to stop the incest because of fears of impregnating his mother (though such fears could have been present), but rather that the mother stopped the incest when her son was no longer 'the ideal partner' or, shall I say, the part-object ideally designed for her perverse purposes. As soon as the boy behaved like an adult and achieved ejaculation, she no longer felt in control of the situation. She was now, in her mind and body, with a man and therefore — in her fantasies — at his mercy.

In the range of female perversions, where do the incest cases fit? It seems that the incest offender attacks her offspring, but simultaneously she is encircling, engulfing, and not letting her victim go. Is it this quality of possessiveness that makes Shengold ask '. . . is the sexualization of the craving for human contact that can lead to incest and perversion a healthier turn [for the child] than the arrest of emotional and sexual development?' (1980, p. 464). However, in my experience, incest and perverting attitudes themselves lead to the arrest of emotional and sexual development. Action and response are not incompatible, but complementary. Victims of either incest or perversion show crippling and lasting effects in their emotional and sexual development; case after case bears this out.

Sperling, in remarking upon the aetiology of fetishism in children, says that 'in the lives of these children there has been *real* seduction and actual overstimulation of these component instincts in the relationship with the parents, especially with the *mother*' (1963, p. 381, my italics).

In all cases of maternal incest described by Kramer (1980) and Margolis (1980), the referrals for treatment had been made because of the children's behaviour. In other words, the children became patients because of the parents' increasing worries about their child's aggressive behaviour. (It is interesting how often maternal incest comes to light only when the children begin to show open violence. Until fear enters in, secrecy is maintained because of the mother's collusion.) This strange situation becomes almost grotesque in the case described by Margolis in which the mother of a twenty-seven-year-old male was first seen by a psychiatrist because she complained that he had sexually assaulted her. She also claimed that he had threatened to kill her and her boyfriend with a shotgun. The patient had had sexual intercourse with his mother for three years before his arrest.

Although his mother admitted to only four acts of intercourse, the patient conceded to having relations with her at least eighteen to twenty times. Due to his shame at reporting these details, it is doubtful that John inflated this record of sexual experience with his mother. It is more likely that the patient's mother attempted to minimize the true extent of their sexual activities. (p. 268)

Likewise, in the three cases reported by Kramer (1981) the children were taken into psychiatric consultation because of their parents' alarm. In one case the child was brought to analysis because the parents greatly feared the child's aggression; in the other two cases the children so dominated the parents with their tyrannical behaviour that the parents' tolerance of the status quo diminished or disappeared.

It looks as if in all cases reported by both authors the aggression and violence appeared in the victims at a later stage. Most professionals are familiar with the mechanism of projective identification (that is, identification with the aggressor) which emerges in these cases. The perpetrators of seduction of children often have an early history of having been seduced themselves. The pervasive, self-perpetuating quality of perversion and its effects shows itself again and again. In Margolis's case this is painfully clear. In one of the cases that Kramer cites, Abby, a five-year-old victim of her mother's sexual molestation, attempts to recreate with her dog the act of sexual stimulation that her mother had inflicted on her (1980, p. 332). This could be an instance in which a new perversion — bestialism — was introduced in which the dog represented the infantile and undermined parts of herself as seen by her internal mother.

I have similar experience of female patients who have suffered from sexual perversions as a result of a perverse, incestuous relationship with their mothers. Such is the case of Miss E, who was sent to me for consultation because of her compulsion to expose herself sexually to figures of authority, particularly women. This had led her to be expelled from everywhere — schools, training centres, jobs, counselling groups, and even mental hospitals — such was the havoc, puzzlement, and sense of powerlessness she created.

She was a plump, rather plain-looking woman of thirty-four. When I first saw her she appeared to be eager to please, but very scared. She gave me this impression despite the fact that I had previously been warned of her 'dangerousness', meaning her tendency to develop crushes on women in authority and to make an absolute nuisance of herself to the point of pestering previous doctors with letters and phone calls, and even unexpectedly showing up at their home addresses and pursuing them with her exhibitionistic behaviour.

She told me that her compulsion to 'flash' occurred when she became attached to someone whom she invested with idealized 'maternal' qualities. She wanted to get closer to, be noticed by and be taken care of by that particular person, but she also wanted a shocked response from her 'victim'. She was careful always to wear the 'appropriate' gear when she was to meet that person, usually only an overcoat over a little vest, so she could respond readily to her urges. She knew this was wrong and that she would be rejected, but could not stop herself.

She had had this urge since she was very small, but at first was able to contain it. At school she had a crush on one of her female teachers but limited her actions to undressing in her presence. This gave her much sexual pleasure. At the age of seventeen, while being trained in an institution, she developed a crush on the principal and for the first time succumbed to her compulsion. Since then she had been unable to bear the tension and had repeated the same action over and over again with teachers, heads of institutions, doctors, bosses, and so on. Each time this brought disaster. She was expelled from everywhere because of her 'antisocial' behaviour, even by psychiatrists and psychotherapists who could not tolerate it.

On one occasion a victim of hers, an older woman, got furious and slapped her. My patient was surprised at her own reaction, which was one of intense enjoyment and sexual excitement. She then very quickly 'learnt' that what she wanted most from these 'mother-figures' was to be either masturbated or slapped on the bottom by them. The referral letter stated that her actions seemed to be in response to masochistic needs rather than being aimed at sexual relationships. She had never had a close relationship, emotionally or physically, with either sex. She had lived in institutions from the age of eight as pupil, trainee, employee, or in-patient.

It was not difficult to believe her own account of being masturbated by her mother from a very early age every time she felt sad or upset or to make her go to sleep, and her account was confirmed when her mother was interviewed. The mother had masturbated not only this little girl, but also her other four children. In the mother's own words, 'it was easier than to use a dummy'. She said that at the time she felt depressed as she was in an unhappy marriage to a man who used to get drunk and beat her up constantly. She also admitted that these actions with her children gave her an enormous sense of comfort and elation. It was also the only way she could make herself go to sleep. She showed no psychotic features.

My patient, like all perverse patients, had used splitting, projective identification, and sexualization as a survival kit in dealing with the outside world. She was employing manic defences in an attempt to deal with her intense, chronic, masked depression which resulted from a very deprived childhood, in which she was made to feel a part or continuation of her mother's body, existing only to provide her mother with narcissistic and sexual gratification. She was literally 'something' located between her thighs that mother would touch, caress, or rub: whenever the patient felt like crying, that was the only way to pacify her. Life required little more of her than her response to this repetitive, incessant and restless motion. And in this she was not on her own, as all her siblings were simultaneously living through the same experience. She later learnt that her way of survival was communal living, where the law lay with the principal and no independence or self-assertion were permitted, while making as little trouble as possible among her peer group. The next move in her strategy was to develop a crush for the female principal who, like mother, would then use her. She was giving herself as a sacrificial victim in order to keep everybody together in harmony.

Her hope for a shocked response in her victims had to do with a hopeful outcome in which women in authority — symbolic mothers — would not respond like her own mother, using and exploiting her as a part-object, but still she had to test them to the extreme. By pestering them through letters, phone calls, and visits to their 'private' homes, she was in deep projective identification with her own mother's intrusiveness into her own 'private' parts. She felt justified in so doing, since this had been done to her. She had now become the aggressor; she even saw herself as such by her own admission that what she was doing was wrong, though she could not help doing it.

So, as usual, behind her perverse actions lay the hope of a magic, hopeful outcome. She longed to escape from her traumatic experiences as a child, yet her actions were imbued with such perverse psychopathology, borrowed from her mother, that she also sought total revenge. No emotional relationships had ever populated her inner world.

It is interesting to note that, even though her exhibitionism appeared superficially to be the equivalent of male 'flashing', this is not so. It is well known that male exhibitionists have the compulsion to 'flash' only at women — and women who are unknown to them, while my patient would expose herself only to other women she felt closely attached to. This is yet another remarkable difference between the genders (see Chapter 2).

Another patient was sent to me for consultation because of a wide range of problems, which included a feeling of extreme disgust at the thought of being touched by anybody in any way. The idea of sexual relationships was abhorrent to her; even seeing other people touch each other was nauseating. She also had suicidal impulses of a highly compulsive quality, which often made her feel obliged to stay in bed. She had severe eating problems, alternating between fasting and binges which sometimes led to vomiting. While eating she sometimes experienced intrusive images, for example that the grapefruit she was eating was her dead mother's brains, or that she was eating other parts of her mother, whereupon she would vomit forth the dead flesh. She saw herself as exceptionally ugly and fat (in fact she was extremely good-looking). Sometimes she used to masturbate compulsively for hours, most often after vomiting. She was deeply disgusted by her masturbation. She was often too frightened to go out to face other people, and consequently was unable to work regular hours.

She was the only child of a broken marriage, and was brought up by her mother alone from a very early age. Her mother was intrusive to the point of never leaving her by herself. The patient talked of herself as a non-entity, 'just a part of my mother', unable to make decisions. She hated her legs because they were the same shape as her mother's (or were they mother's?). She still remembered vividly how mother used to get into bed with her at night, cried a lot and made her promise never to leave her alone. If she promised, mother would 'reward' her by touching her all over, especially around her thighs, which would make her feel very excited. This happened nearly every night.

Kramer states that incestuous mothers have never allowed their children any sense of individuation. (Perhaps one of the reasons why the 'Jocasta complex' was never identified as such is that she gave up Oedipus from the moment of his birth.) Kramer considers 'maternal incest to be more than an inadvertence: it is the mother's repetitive, deliberate actions, aimed at stimulating the child to gratify herself. The child may be male or female' (1980, p. 328). I suggest that when Kramer defines her concept of 'maternal incest', she is actually describing a type of female perversion.

In the above descriptions we can see some of the conditions which characterize a perversion, such as repetition and the compulsive element in sexual gratification through the reduction of object to part-object. Another characteristic is dehumanization, as described in the following passage from the same paper: 'I speculate that they [incestuous mothers] could not enjoy their own genitals for sexual pleasure, but masturbated the genitals of their incompletely separated and individuated children as dehumanized extensions of the maternal body' (p. 330). Kramer also suggests that these mothers were homosexuals. This quality of dehumanization was vividly described by my patient who identified her child with various parts of her own body (see above, pp. 72–3). Kramer concentrates on maternal incest, and poses a similar question to mine about female perversions, especially in connection with motherhood: 'Why are authors so loath to label sexual stimulation by the mother as incest, and relatively ready to acknowledge paternal incest?' She offers as a possible explanation the idea that 'the resistance to the concept of "maternal incest" is related to the deep-seated, almost universal split between mother as madonna and whore' (p. 328).

My clinical observations confirm this bias. On countless occasions agencies and establishments have shown signs of alarm, sometimes almost panic, when referring male patients to me as sexual abusers. This contrasts strongly with the difficulty my female patients have often had in being taken seriously by some agencies. The few women who eventually refer themselves to me for treatment do so because they are hoping to find someone prepared to make the effort to understand their feelings of being too close emotionally and physically to their child, whether boy or girl. I have noticed that mothers are more ready to report incestuous feelings and actions towards their daughters than towards their sons. In the latter case one does not get to know until much later, and then usually from the son's history.

In this context I remember a patient of mine who was originally referred from a child guidance clinic where her daughter, aged six, had been sent because of behavioural problems mainly related to school refusal. Following diagnostic assessment there, it was decided that the girl's problems were the result of a very disturbed and difficult family situation, particularly her relationship with her mother.

My patient was described as an inadequate mother who showed intense exhibitionistic behaviour, such as exaggerating her physical demonstrations of affection towards her daughter. However, when she had decided some time before to seek a consultation for herself because of these preoccupations, she was told not to worry; and that 'it is just natural for a mother to feel very fond of her children, especially if she is a single parent'. She had identified so closely with her daughter that she had come to act like a little girl herself, expecting her daughter to take complete care of her needs, including being cuddled and bathed by her. The little girl defended herself against these excessive demands by a most primitive and infantile acting-out.

Mother and daughter had created a symbiotic relationship to the extent of sharing the same bed. The mother had initiated the girl in active sexual incest which progressed from having her breasts caressed to her masturbating her daughter's genitals. The mother had not allowed the girl to attend school because she could not bear the idea of her being away. Nor would she let her have her own friends, or life, or allow her to grow up.

My patient explained:

I want to be the mother I never had, someone who could be all the time with me and whose attentions could be entirely devoted to me as her daughter instead of being like my mother, hating me so much for being a girl and so involved with the other children and her husband that she never had a minute for me alone. She never forgave me, either, that I was born a girl, being the first child. She had so much longed for a boy. I was always the victim of humiliation, and it became much worse when all the other children, five, were born. They were all girls. Then my mother turned to me with even more hatred than ever. [This patient was born into a culture in which women were considered as social inferiors (much more overtly than in the UK) and had very little opportunity to make a life of their own.] As soon as I could I emigrated to this country with the purpose of making my own life as a 'woman'.

Thereafter my patient became a prostitute, a profession she felt offered her the opportunity of being valued for her female body, whereas previously she had felt degraded because of it. According to her, she felt a kick of elation not only that her body was desired by men, but also that they were ready to pay for it. Also, she was able to bring another dimension to her job through her intelligence, her wonderful command of language, and her skilled powers of communication, all of which had long been so overlooked. She became such an expert storyteller that sometimes she could pocket her clients' money without it ever occurring to them to touch her body, so mesmerized were they by her erotic tales. She too drew some comfort from her stories, as they temporarily relieved her intense feelings of depression and low self-esteem. But this proved not to be enough. Her hidden, suppressed despair and despondency began to emerge in a way which she felt unable to contain. There was a raging, sad little girl within her, who demanded furiously to be taken care of.

Eventually she decided to have a child, through which her own expectations of childhood would be fulfilled. The man chosen for this project had merely to impregnate her. She had even forgotten who he was; perhaps, though, she felt happier at not acknowledging him, because she was scared to have as father to her child someone like her own father, who not only had totally ignored her after her birth, but later hindered her development and denied her the academic achievement of which she was clearly capable. She had only contempt towards her mother, primarily because she had felt so rejected by her for being a girl. How could she come to terms with having a body like her mother's and leading a life like her mother's? After all, as a woman, marrying and having children would be to follow in her mother's footsteps. How could she overcome those feelings of self-deprecation which she had been so used to for so long? She had experienced her mother as an object of her father's contempt for producing only girls, a sex so much underrated by both of them.

My patient was a highly intelligent and sensitive woman who had never felt any encouragement as a human being, let alone as a girl. She had never trusted anyone and had always kept aloof. Her clients had become 'her only friends'; all men, they were never really friends. This she knew. Now her search was for someone she could trust and who would be completely dependent on her. Who knows what might have happened had her child been a boy and not a girl? But she had a girl. In her daughter she saw a reflection of herself and her own needs. She viewed herself, to start with, as an excellent mother. She spent all her time with her daughter, as her working hours never interfered with her functioning as a mother: she would only work at night, when the child was asleep. So it was only when the daughter began to have emotional problems that the mother started a long and laborious questioning of her own motivations. She had so much wanted her daughter to have everything that she had never had herself, and had been so determined to make enough money for the girl not to suffer the same deprivations, that she became overwhelmed by the unexpected conflicts she now experienced. This was when treatment began.

The institution, if it can be called that, of substitute motherhood throws some light on why we have been so alert to the dangers of paternal incest while being so blind to those of maternal incest. 'Incest' with a substitute mother is quite frequent in the past where a woman fulfilling a domestic task (a maid or a cook perhaps) initiates the young boy of the house into sexual life as he reaches puberty. The boy responds gratefully, and is later able to exercise his newly acquired techniques confidently with his coevals. This 'benevolent' act is very different from a substitute father initiating a young girl into sex. In the former case society turns a blind eye; in the latter it shouts its outrage. Is this because of the myth that mothers are madonnas and therefore untouched by sexuality except for procreation? The participation of the maid (cleaner) or cook (provider of earthly food) is appropriate in both concrete and symbolic terms. She is the one who can indulge in acts of sexuality which are seen as dirty and shameful by those particular societies but domestically and socially acceptable, due to her 'lesser' position. She not only initiates the young boy into sexuality, but is also seen as securing the mother's 'holy' position.

However, as we observe again and again, the real mother's incestuous behaviour towards her son usually causes him to develop a polymorphous–perverse sexual psychopathology. Rinsley described the treatment of a patient of his who used to visit prostitutes, and was sexually potent only if he felt 'nothing' for the woman; as soon as any loving feelings appeared he became impotent. According to Rinsley, 'the impotency served the interrelated functions of preserving the symbiotic tie to the borderline mother and warding off her "real" rivals' (1978, p. 52). The patient had an early history of being genitally masturbated by his mother at bathtime since the age of six, just before starting primary school, a manoeuvre obviously designed to continue her seduction and prolong his dependency on and symbiosis with her. I believe this mother was perverse and not borderline. We shall become familiar with similar problems in Chapter 6, in which the 'split object-relations unit' so termed by Masterson and Rinsley (1975) is at work in both parties, or rather in the self and the object.

Whal (1960) reports two cases of mother–son incest which led the sons to become schizophrenic. According to Whal, in the Oedipus complex 'unconscious fear is not just of the powerful, retributive, castrating father, but also of the all-encompassing mother who gives not only the breast but takes, as the female spider takes — leaving the hollow husk of her mate as a memento of their ecstasy' (p. 192). I find this statement useful, though it seems more of a denigration of women than an attempt to understand their predicaments. Whal then adds that: 'Incestuous problems in schizophrenic patients play a much larger role in the development of schizophrenia than had hitherto been supposed' (p. 192).

Society's different responses to maternal and paternal incest may be related to inaccessible processes operating in the unconscious mind of both men and women, starting from early life. From the moment of conception women go through obvious physical changes. Both men and women experience a strange world of conscious and unconscious fantasies about conception, gestation, and childbirth. Pregnancy not only transforms the woman's body, but also creates expectations about herself, her baby, her object-relationships, and her personal circumstances; all this, except for the bodily changes, takes place in the man's mind too. We could therefore say that the baby exists before it is born.

The main concern has been with the baby's fantasies, its perceptions of the world, and its ability to create images of its own. Parents' perceptions of their baby and the many implications the birth has for their world are being revised, especially in view of the incidence of incest from parents who were themselves incest victims. In fact, their own childhood, especially how their own parents treated them, will determine their attitude to the newborn. In studying them we can learn more about the psychogenic factors in perversion, and gain some insight into the marked differences in response to paternal and maternal incest.

The mother is so obviously close to the baby, biologically and emotionally, that no ambivalence or hostility towards it is expected from her. The father is considered to be much more distant from the infant, and is thus seen as exploiting his own power when taking advantage of his child's body and mind. Whereas society acknowledges paternal incest as some males' way of dealing with their insecurities, it tends to overlook their deep motivations. These insecurities are often rooted in infancy and are linked with the man's feelings about motherhood arising from his relationship with his own mother, feelings which are later reactivated by his partner's pregnancy.

Why, then, is it so hard to believe in maternal incest, or to regard it as being as serious as male incest? Even in group therapy, which offers a microcosm of society where this phenomenon is mirrored, men and women alike tend to express not only concern but also shock when confronted with male offenders. They seem to identify with the little girls, and view the father's actions with revulsion and repulsion. In fact this can prove therapeutic since male offenders are shamed as they would be in society (though as accepted group members, these reactions are less punitive). After a period of intolerance, group members often show concern and care.

By contrast, the female 'offender' finds that other patients minimize her problems. Nobody wants to hear about her predicament, and nobody takes her very seriously. This reaction proves very anti-therapeutic, and if the therapist is not ready to interpret this total denial for them, these women will never gain any insight into their problems, let alone be able to change themselves.

The aetiology of perversion, I believe, is intertwined with the politics of power; one aspect is psychobiological and the other social. It is possible that this difference of response is

caused by society's inability to see woman as a complete human   105
being. The difficulties in acknowledging that mothers can
abuse their power could be the result of total denial, as a way of
dealing with this unpalatable truth. Woman is seen as a part-
object, a mere receptacle for man's perverse designs. The
apparent idealization with which society hides female perverse
attitudes ('Women don't do those awful things') actually
contains a denigrating counterpart. Until recently a lack of
legislation on female perversion reflected society's total denial
of it.

The study of power politics might throw new light on the
understanding of motherhood functions. Perhaps if women
had a longer tradition of belonging to the power structure their
attitudes to men and children would not be governed, as they
are now, by a weakness which they strive to turn into
possessiveness and control.

MOTHERS
WHO COMMIT
INCEST

6 THE SYMBOLIC MOTHER
AS A WHORE:
Whose Control is it Anyway?

F EMALE PROSTITUTION involves both sexes, and the
men as well as the women have problems that are not
always obvious. In more ways than one double standards
are at work. This is not surprising since a contract based on
money is entered into, and the two parties are in some ways
accomplices, in other ways opponents. They have different
expectations of what is ostensibly just a physical act, but in
reality has many symbolic associations. Cultural, sociological
and economic factors are interlinked with deep emotional
motivations.

It is impossible to comprehend the phenomenon of prostitution by looking just at the prostitute herself, or just at the
man who pursues her. A dynamic process is at work, an
interaction between two people each with their own history,
their own present circumstances, and their separate need to
establish some equilibrium which they hope will be obtained
through this contract. Outsiders or critics may view prostitution as precarious, wrong or immoral, but obviously both
prostitute and client see it as a way of fulfilling a need, and
both hope for a successful and complementary outcome.

According to my clinical findings, the fact that prostitute and client are anonymous, strangers with no emotional commitment to each other, appears to be the most important aspect of prostitution. This strangeness can provide each partner both with unlimited fantasy material (for example of belonging to the other gender) and with the 'safety' inherent in the avoidance of intimate relationships, emotional or otherwise. Without such implications the differentiation of the sexes and the achievement of a true object-relationship is impossible. But let us not forget that a financial transaction is taking place, and that it will affect the fantasies of each party.

We are familiar with the double standards the law seems to apply. These can work both ways for either sex leaving both in an unequal position. Whereas colleagues have been overconcerned with the intrapsychic functions of men who go to prostitutes, this has rarely been acknowledged by the legal system. Legal statistics reveal an enormous difference between the number of women who appear in court on charges of prostitution and the near absence of their male counterparts, the kerb-crawlers, who are almost never charged. Thus, despite the lip-service which has been paid to the intrapsychic dysfunction in men who are not only ready to pay for prostitutes' services but will roam the streets to look for them, 'legal help' (detection) is not made available to them. In other words, although men are 'let off the hook', they are not being understood by the law. If it is assumed that the legal system should operate for both the safety of the citizens and the welfare of the offenders, this leaves men in an unequal position. Unlike women, the men can offer no socio-economical excuse: they are evidently able to afford the services of prostitutes, while some women who practise prostitution, say, do so for financial reasons.

Some researchers have claimed that women who engage in prostitution do so only for socio-economic reasons, overlooking their emotional problems; others have claimed the opposite — that the only problems these women have are emotional ones. My main concern, however, is with the double standard which has allowed us to believe that while women have gone into prostitution as a means of overcoming

THE SYMBOLIC
MOTHER AS
A WHORE

emotional problems, the same is not true for men. In fact, my clinical experience suggests that in many ways both the women and their clients are reacting, though in different ways, to their early experiences with their mothers. Before examining the evidence for this contention, let us first consider a few explanations for prostitution put forward by authors from different schools of thought.

Why is it that prostitution is a much more frequent phenomenon in women than in men? As Grunberger reminds us, 'Freud insisted that the narcissistic woman wants "to be loved". To be loved means primarily to be chosen, and above all to be loved for herself. Without doubt there are many reasons for this, including the need to free herself from conflict-producing guilt, on which Chasseguet-Smirgel has remarked . . . but this is only one aspect of female narcissism.' Grunberger goes further, saying: 'We must try to understand why women seek narcissistic gratification above all else, even to the detriment of their strong sexual needs, and why they offer themselves sexually in order to be loved; whereas men tend to seek sexual gratification primarily (men love in order to be satisfied)' (1985, p. 70).

Kinsey *et al.* offer the simplistic explanation that 'Men go to prostitutes because they can pay for the sexual relations and forget other responsibilities, whereas coitus with other girls may involve them socially and legally beyond anything which they care to undertake' (1948, p. 607).

Krout Tabin goes further: 'We can see, however, that additionally responsibility for sex can be equated with ties to the love-object and that to a man who has not solidified his ego-core such closeness threatens engulfment' (1985, p. 92). She describes clearly the male pattern and the unconscious motivations of men who seek prostitutes, but she fails to do the same for women who engage in prostitution.

Coria has pointed out 'that in our culture money is clearly sexualized and associated with manhood and virility'. According to her, 'prostitution is considered synonymous with a woman selling her sexuality, but it curiously omits the man who buys it' (1986, p. 23, my translation).

Simone de Beauvoir says that 'In prostitution, male desire

can be satisfied on no matter what body, such desire being specific but not individualized as to object' (1972, p. 569). She would seem to be describing a part-object relationship which is characteristic of perverse relations, but she fails to make the same observation for women.

According to Gibbens (1957), women who engage in prostitution have a wish to turn men into swine as a revenge for a traumatic childhood. He has named this the 'Circe complex' (p. 7).

Glover (1943) says that it is impossible to study the problem of prostitution in isolation since, like all sexual problems, it is two-sided and only part of the wider role of sexuality in human affairs. He adds that the sexual life of both prostitute and client contains a marked component of sadism, either manifest or latent, whose injurious consequences indicate an unconscious masochistic component in which mutual depreciation is the rule.

Rolph (1955) develops Glover's comprehensive analysis of female prostitution when he argues that the desire to debase the sexual partner is not exclusive to women. He maintains that the male client has a need to debase the woman or mother-figure, and that the prostitute serves this purpose. Consequently a symbiotic relationship is created in which the prostitute's and the client's pathological needs are each satisfied.

It is my suggestion that at times both men and women engaged in prostitution unconsciously re-enact an early mother–boy relationship in which both are concerned with the symbolism of bodily ministrations, more precisely with his toilet-training. There is a general assumption that the services provided by a prostitute are exclusively sexual, but this is not so, as appears from the accounts of many women who have engaged in prostitution, and also of men who pay for these services. Not infrequently a 'supportive' or 'reassuring' meeting occurs with very little or no physical contact. However, money is always involved. A clear contract is made: the woman states the price which the man has to pay for the 'goods' to be produced. She has the upper hand in these transactions, which are symbolically associated with anality, the control of the sphincter, and therefore with the flow of his emotionality.

THE SYMBOLIC
MOTHER AS
A WHORE

Krout Tabin has some illuminating comments to make about the whore/madonna complex when she describes a two-year-old boy as feeling in danger from his sexual urges towards his mother, and pushes them away, so splitting the mother into two halves. One half offers support but not sexuality, while to the other half he can react sexually without being pushed. Both halves afford him the illusion of being close, but not too close. This split in adulthood can express itself in sexual impotence involving the 'part-object' use of the penis. As Krout Tabin observes, 'the man's penis seems independent of his will' (1985, p. 92).

Many people may be surprised at the sense of bewilderment and despair felt by some men who frequent prostitutes. It can reach such a pitch that they seek psychiatric help. Let us look at some of these men's problems.

Mr R, an attractive, intelligent, thirty-eight-year-old married man, a successful professional in the arts, came to see me because of his compulsive need to visit prostitutes. The better his marriage went, the worse this had become. This had brought him much unhappiness since, he said, he loved his wife very much and had a most satisfactory sexual relationship with her. Therefore he was unable to understand this 'bizarre obsession'. He felt full of shame and was puzzled by it, particularly since he had been consistently unable to perform sexually with prostitutes. Even though 'it may sound irrational', he felt the reason for this had to do with his ability to have 'good sex' with his wife. He saw the latter as directly linked to his compulsion to visit prostitutes.

During the course of psychotherapy his enormous sense of insecurity emerged clearly, as well as his tremendous fear of being left alone and his inability to trust anyone. For a long time he had a strong feeling that I would abruptly stop treatment because he was not worthy of it, and he feared/hoped to be humiliated by me in all sorts of ways. He was trying to behave like the perfect child, but was reluctant to talk about his problems. In the transferential interpretations he tried very hard to struggle against accepting that, superficially, his

motivation for treatment had to do with replacing 'acting-in' for 'acting-out'. In other words, he had secretly hoped that by

becoming my patient and paying for my professional services,
this would magically 'cure' him of his need to pay prostitutes
for their services. Thus his psychotherapy would replace his
perversion.

Whereas at the start I assumed, in transferential terms, that
his fears belonged to an early oral stage in which he might have
felt neglected or under a threat of separation from his mother, I
soon became aware that his fears belonged to the later anal
stage and his relationship to his mother during his toilet-
training. The evidence emerged clearly enough. He spoke of his
'messing around', which he felt I would be very critical of, for
he 'knew' that the 'goods' he was supposed to deliver to me,
were in fact being delivered elsewhere. All the 'dirty, smelly
stuff' had to be dealt with by the prostitutes. I had become the
tyrannical mother who expected him to be clean at all times
and to 'obey my commands'. It was not unusual for him in this
period of his therapy to visit a prostitute either on the way to
his sessions or on the way back. He then would arrive full of
shame to 'confess' to me, again in the hope/dread of being
rejected and so being able to continue this painful but familiar
pattern. At other times, in complaining of his wife's inability
to please him with his sexual fantasies, he saw me as his sadistic
father telling him how small and inadequate he was in dealing
with his mother's 'moods'.

Later on, though, he became painfully aware of his deeply
ingrained hatred towards his mother. Persistently, from his
earliest days, he had felt emotionally wounded by her and also
used by her in her constant rows with his father, so much so
that he did not know who he really was. He was unable to
visualize himself as a father, such was his fear of becoming like
his own father and of the prospective child becoming like
himself. He was so vulnerable to and dependent on his mother,
and so afraid of her power to abuse him, that his hatred led to
visits to prostitutes. He divided women into two sorts:
madonna and whore. As a matter of fact, the 'irrational
reasons' mentioned in his first interview were quite valid. He
was protecting his marriage and indeed his wife from his
fantasied sadistic attacks on his mother, and now on me. This
was more acceptable to him than the fearful risk of trusting in

THE SYMBOLIC
MOTHER AS
A WHORE

112 just one person and failing to come up to that person's expectations. Frequenting prostitutes was his only way to protect himself from all those inner demands and the consequent psychological injuries. In his own words, 'to experience the joy of love one must be vulnerable and able to trust; I am too childish and too selfish for that'.

Another patient, a single man of twenty-eight, came for treatment because of his inability to establish a satisfactory relationship with a woman. He looked for perfection. Nobody 'is good enough for me', was his statement. He was a successful businessman who couldn't believe in his 'good luck'; nevertheless he felt unable to compete with his father, who had worked his way up from nothing. This constantly made him feel inadequate and useless. He was an only child, and was cautious in talking about his mother, whom he described as a most beautiful woman. After some time in treatment he was able to talk — albeit reluctantly — about his search for prostitutes.

This patient was handsome, well spoken, and had some superficial charm, but underneath it all he was extremely domineering and unbending and, despite his claims of being compassionate and considerate, he could at times become sadistic in his relentless search for perfection and cleanliness. This became obvious during therapy, when he would comment on any changes in either my consulting room or my person. He would suddenly switch for no apparent reason from absolute idealization to complete denigration. Whenever he got emotionally close to me, he would see me as an attractive woman and fantasize about me in sexual terms. This would suddenly change into severe vilification conducted in a pitiless, determined and obstinate manner. At the beginning, he said, he had found me ugly and repulsive. All this material was treated in the transference and he would get more and more cross with me.

It was obvious that the patient was trying to destroy my therapeutic skills during an intense period of negative therapeutic reaction by making highly provocative statements.

Eventually he succeeded, by making hostile remarks about my standards of hygiene, highly marked with anality and mostly

related to smells. I was supposed to 'stink', to have bad breath,
to have terrible body odour. The remarks were extended to the
condition of my consulting room: 'it's tarty', 'the heater is
leaking', or perhaps 'it has to do with your farting in the room'.
His stubbornness had no equal. He had by now begun to win
his battle, by making me feel furious and impotent in my anger.
Any attempt at my interpreting his projective identification
and his own internal bad objects thrown at me was met with
derision and laughter. I realized these episodes amounted to a
re-enactment of his own toilet-training and the bitter fight
during that period of his life with his mother. Moreover, I saw
that he had succeeded in making me feel just as he must have
felt as a small child confronted by his mother about his lack of
cleanliness. (I had reacted in 'complementary identification',
in Kernberg's terminology (1980, p. 212). I found Kernberg's
paper on technique extremely revealing and most helpful in
working through my countertransference with such patients.)

When he heard this interpretation, my patient's mood
changed from derision to intense despair. He talked of his
mother having had fourteen miscarriages before his own birth.
He produced fantasies associated with his belief that his
mother had been a practising prostitute before her marriage to
his father. His associations with my consulting room and
myself had to do with very primitive fantasies about his
mother's reproductive organs, how inadequate and dirty they
had been that they had produced so many deaths before his own
birth. By now he felt deeply contaminated, and it was from his
own body that all this poison emanated because he felt it was
uncontainable. His initial statement, 'Nothing or nobody is
good enough for me', was a projection of his own worth-
lessness, and his search for prostitutes reflected a secret
unconscious wish to be in fusion with his mother, whom he
both hated and loved. To be reborn was felt by him to be his
only solution.

Krout Tabin describes a two-year-old boy's behaviour as his
own way of defining the 'bad' self, as opposed to being
engulfed by the 'good' mother. She adds: 'The value of
negativism to prove separateness extends to express frustration
and anger in his ambivalent wish for closeness to his mother.

THE SYMBOLIC
MOTHER AS
A WHORE

114 Sexuality thus becomes confused with terror and anger and, at the extreme of negativism, the inflicting of pain and taking complete control over the other. To control seems the opposite of engulfment' (1985, p. 92). I find this description comparable to what occurs in prostitution, not only in the man who is pursuing prostitutes but also in the symbolism of the transaction itself. My patient mentioned above was behaving like a toddler, defying me to enter a situation of power, and hoping to leave me impotent and full of rage, feeling utterly useless in my therapeutic aims. However, I was eventually able to understand his predicament and thus regained my own therapeutic skills.

I have often wondered whether some women, in becoming mothers of toddlers, are more demanding or more instrusive with their sons' than with their daughters' toilet-training, since some of the character traits often associated with this stage of development, such as stubbornness, defiance, and competitiveness, appear more frequently in men than in women. Is it possible that the position of control over the controlling orifices and waste products of young children of the opposite gender could generate the curiosity and excitement responsible for this different attitude and its subsequent outcome? Or could it be that girls are able to complete their toilet-training more quickly in view of the different development of the libido?

In prostitution both parties are seeking control, but whose control is it anyway? To start with, there is the false assumption that the encounter is necessarily a sexual-genital one. I believe that both parties are involved in some compromise whereby the sexual mother is being taken over by the strict mother, provider of bodily ministrations. The woman is clearly in charge of the initial contract and, in some cases, of the outcome too. However, the man shares the same expectation. In his view, since he pays he is in charge, and he knows exactly what the outcome will be. He pays for the illusion that he won't be taken over by an all-invading mother, and therefore he feels safe.

The man is now reduced to the state of 'a good boy' who has delivered the 'goods', money (faeces), to an 'anal' mother in order to satisfy and gratify her whimsical needs. He wants to believe that he is now ready for sexual gratification, but actually he behaves as if defying his mother in toilet-training. Glover (1943) talks of prostitution as a debased form of love, and reminds us that unconsciously money is equated with the excretory products of the body, which children regard as precious possessions. He also acknowledges that

the man who has compulsive interest in prostitutes is still fixated to his old profane love and seeks, without knowing it, to gratify in adult life the tabooed desires of infancy. For her part the prostitute has similar unconscious aims, but their scope is more ambitious. The client, the 'strange man' who pays for her favours, is the deteriorated image of her father; at the same time, she registers her violently jealous disapproval of her mother's marriage by, as it were, debasing her own feminine currency. (p. 5)

The fact that the woman is trading her body for 'filthy lucre is in fact one more proof that prostitution is a primitive and regressive manifestation' (p. 7). It looks to me as if Glover is close to indicating that the man, in pursuing prostitutes, is looking for a mother he desired as a forbidden sexual object. But, unable to obtain this sexual gratification, he has had to content himself with a substitute maternal denigrated figure who belongs to a regressed anal libidinal phase.

Furthermore, a process of projective identification takes place within both parties' minds in an attempt to resolve this primitive splitting. The prostitute now becomes in fantasy a mother with a young child — her client — submissive under her control; simultaneously she is also a whore who is supposed to provide that 'youngster' with sexual gratification. This is made possible by a process of depersonalization, and by a mutual and reciprocal splitting and the denial of emotions which occurs as a result. The process also involves a generational confusion, as envisaged by Chasseguet-Smirgel (1985a) when she talks of the anal universe in perversion where all differences are abolished, differences about sexes and about generations. In prostitution the woman at times becomes a mother and the man a child. At other times the client becomes 'the dirty old man', with connotations of dirt associated with money, faeces corresponding to a pre-oedipal stage. At other times, he is the 'sugar daddy', easily associated with orality, sugar and milk; in other words, a mother who is able to feed the woman/baby to satisfy any whimsical needs she might have. As Sayers (1986) has reminded us, 'Irrespective of its sex, the child seeks to repeat not only the active but also the passive aspects of the anal as well as oral pleasures it derives from, or "produced" in it by, its interactions with those who first look after the physical needs associated with these pleasures.' She adds that, 'despite the cultural associations of scoptophilia with masculinity . . . girls also seek to repeat the voyeuristic pleasure, as they experience it, of the one who supervises the toilet. Like boys they too contrive to watch others at their toilet' (pp. 105–6).

In any case, a pre-oedipal perverse dyadic process (mother, child) is at work, and the associated degree of risk demands a process of triangulation which is offered by a strict and punitive superego: the law — a symbolic father who is called upon to perform his duties. He is expected to extricate both parties from a perverse, unhealthy association and to create some sense of order. In other words, prostitute and client are re-enacting an 'ideal', illusory, and collusive situation in which the symbolic mother–baby unit tries to get away without the husband/father, but simultaneously they are both knowingly challenging the law/husband/father with a possible prosecution. But the father colludes with his own gender in the application of the law: the woman is charged, but the man and his emotional predicaments are dismissed.

If we attempt to examine what goes on in the woman's mind and body while she is with her client, we soon find that it cannot be explained by just one pattern. In fact the process, both consciously and unconsciously, is extremely complicated. My contention is that prostitute and client become partners in minds and bodies in a vengeful and denigrating action against mother. This intimate, anonymous complicity provides both with some gratification and reassurance. Each partner shares the same split view of woman in the whore/madonna complex. The woman leaves all emotions aside when she works as a prostitute, and is able, most of the time, to operate with skill and in complete detachment. The same woman, though, can react with much emotion, tenderness, and care in her relationships outside her work. There, unfortunately, she tends to fall into sadomasochistic relationships in which she is exploited and frequently beaten up by her partner. I think that her tendency to masochism is also represented in man in his relationships with his significant Others when unable to perform sexually. His impotence works both ways: it is an expression of his sadistic needs against his loved ones, but it also puts him in a position where he can easily be humiliated and belittled.

Sometimes prostitution exists only in fantasy; at other times it is real, but even then sexual intercourse does not necessarily take place. For some men the main, unconscious motivation for the visit is to be mesmerized into a blissful state in which they feel safe.

Thus I maintain that the problems of prostitution are not exclusively female ones, though they affect women's internal and external worlds more frequently. Perhaps it would be more accurate to speak in the plural, of 'prostitutions', since a many-levelled process is at work: some women fantasize and daydream about many aspects of becoming a prostitute, and others act upon the fantasies and make a living out of it.

The main characteristics in women who are practising prostitutes might superficially appear to be hostility and contempt towards men, but their self-neglect and the risks to which they expose their bodies are undeniable. These risks are not exclusively physical; they relate also to fantasies involving the mental representations of their bodies.

Such fantasies operate in both concrete and symbolic ways, and have features corresponding to the women's intense depression and self-denigration. Their self-esteem is very low, and in order to get out of this 'low' they start to solicit. When men appear and are ready to pay for their services they feel enormously elated. These women now feel wanted in a direct way. They find this abominable, but simultaneously they feel that their bodies are the only valuable goods they possess. It is unfortunate that in thinking so they are not alone.

THE SYMBOLIC
MOTHER AS
A WHORE

Soliciting, then, is used as a 'regulator of self-esteem' as described by I. Rosen for perversions in general when he says: 'The quality of self-experiences in perversion may vary enormously and exist contradictorily so that a sense of inferiority (resulting from a depleted self) may supplement notions of omnipotence' (1979b, p. 67).

I have heard statements such as this coming from a woman who was due to appear in court for soliciting:

I feel rotten, but what else could I do? I came from the North where nobody ever wanted me, they had been expecting a boy. So I came to London and began to pick up men in the streets. I've appeared several times in court for the same reason. Men are always so nice, they treat me like a normal human being. Every time I feel depressed, I go and I feel much better if a man accepts me. I charge very little but I feel so much more of a woman.

A woman consulted me for depression, suicidal feelings and a general sense of being 'lost in the world'. She was forty-three years old, an attractive woman who may once have been beautiful but who had seen rough times. She had been a practising prostitute for many years, and had appeared in court several times because of violence to others and soliciting in the streets. At the age of seventeen she had been raped, became pregnant, and married the man responsible — a thief who had spent most of his life in prison. At the time of her baby girl's birth, he was once again in prison and unable to provide for her. She felt detached from her baby, and uninterested in her welfare to the point of neglect. Her mother then volunteered to take care of the baby for a while. However, despite my patient's attempts to see her daughter, her mother never let the child go until she too was seventeen, by which time she had become a heroin addict.

My patient described her mother as a 'perfect swine' who was always very contemptuous of her and at the same time passive and uncaring. In her own words, 'My earliest memory of conflict with my mother was her squeezing me with a cushion between us. I was still a baby, but can remember the

intense pressure and my lungs being restricted.' She had always
felt unhappy, singled out at home and at school. After her first
marriage she had many pregnancies by different men, which
was not surprising as she took no precautions, and she kept
aborting herself with a syringe, having done this at least
fourteen times. She added that her compulsive urge for sex led
her to take chances. She was pushed by her husband into
prostitution. She hated him intensely but complied with his
request in the hope that prostitution might have a cheering
effect on her. In a short-lived way it did, but afterwards she felt
more miserable than ever. She tried without success to establish
a relationship with her estranged daughter, who had turned
against her, just as she herself had done with her own mother.
But the daughter was too bitter about her and too preoccupied
with her own problems to allow any relationship to be
established. (Incidentally, the daughter was criticized for this
by a caring boyfriend.) Once more, this patient sought therapy
with a woman in the hope of establishing a good relationship
with a caring mother who could simultaneously deal with her
vengeful feelings.

Her long term of psychotherapy was by no means easy. She
first put me to the test of seduction, and when this failed, she
became angry and confused. A long struggle about separation/
individuation came to the fore, becoming particularly and
painfully apparent during my holidays. How could I care about
her if I could go away and leave her to her own devices, which
were almost non-existent? However, as much pain and distress
as these repeated events caused during psychotherapy, they
eventually proved to have some therapeutic effect on her as she
came to realize that I had my own life and needs, and that I was
there neither to be seduced by her nor to exploit her with my
own emotional demands. Her awareness that I could trust her
to be on her own and that I had my own separate life afforded
her a feeling of freedom to explore her own needs and wants.

Another woman of twenty-eight came to consult me because
of her inability to enjoy sexual intercourse with her husband
since her baby, now aged nine months, had been born. She was
extremely worried about this as she was very fond of her baby's
father, and feared he might get fed up and leave home.

THE SYMBOLIC
MOTHER AS
A WHORE

Later on she told me that she and her husband had been in trouble with the law for many years. He was a professional bank-robber, and she a practising prostitute. They had been able to combine both professions and to get the best out of them while being together. This was a fitting combination, since both in their respective occupations were expressing in a symbolic way their anger at mother and their challenge to father. Her husband, the bank-robber, was getting inside a maternal body, robbing something not belonging to him but to father/bank — a symbol of paternal authority, full of money, virility, and power.

She described their relationship as being the first positive one in her life. They had been able to establish strong bonds to the extent of wanting to have a child of their own. Neither, though, foresaw stopping work, so it was to their chagrin that their son's birth had resulted in turning her off sex altogether. Despite herself, she found sex disgusting either with her husband or with any prospective client. So revolting did she find it that she could not make a career out of it any more, while her sexual relationship with her husband was so precarious that she feared it might result in their separation. Thus both of them, alarmed at her emotional involvement with her baby, faced a major loss in income and also a weakening of their relationship. This was why she had come for consultation.

The patient had an emotionally deprived early history, which partly accounted for her prostitution. She was now unconsciously directing all her cathexis in the direction of her baby through breast-feeding, and feared that if her body were used for any other purpose she would not be able to look after baby adequately, so interfering with his normal development. Evidently motherhood, through an intense identification with her baby and his emotional and physical needs, had provided her with some solution for her previous splitting.

In this particular case I considered that the most suitable option was to offer joint sessions for wife and husband. Sometimes they brought with them the baby, who was occasionally breast-fed. A better understanding of the family dynamics emerged which made it possible for them to remain

income, and she did some part-time work which allowed her to
take care of the baby, and eventually to respond to her
husband's intimate needs. These she no longer saw as conflicting so much with her and her baby's emotional–biological
unit, which by then was also gratifying to her husband.

I believe that the sort of splitting which this patient had
experienced is related to the taboo about maternal incest. If we
recall some of the fantasies during orgasm described in Chapter
2, it would be a massive reality for some women to take inside
their body the baby which had already nested there. Is there a
point of return to the beginning of life? It is like closing a
circuit, birth/death, and the consequence in fantasy is the son's
death. That is why, in a 'detached' way, such a woman allows a
stranger — her client — to attack the inside of her body in a
sadistic way, since loving is absent; only hatred is alive in both
parties. This corresponds to the way she sees herself as
undeserving of any positive feelings for her self-hated body.
Hence, in the process of projective identification with her
client she attacks her own mother's body. But at times, as with
this patient, in becoming a mother herself a process of
identification with an 'ideal' mother occurs. In this case the
image of the 'ideal' mother prevented her from taking risks
with clients. After all, her own sense of self-esteem was at
stake. The birth of this baby had made her feel wanted from
within, with the baby making genuine claims upon her
involving many unexpected emotional and physical gratifications which she did not want to give up.

I have encountered this phenomenon quite often in my
psychotherapeutic work with women who are working as
prostitutes. Despite their emotional deprivation and their
inability to form a female ego-ideal, some of these women have
achieved the creation of a maternal ego-ideal. Regardless of
how inconsistent and erratic it is, this has come to their rescue
in functioning as mothers.

D. Pines reports a similar finding in her treatment of
'normal neurotic' women: 'For some women the birth of the
first child, particularly if it is a male child, may complicate
adult sexual relationships since the mother may have problems

122   in using her body for pleasure with her sexual partner as well as for nurturing. Many women experience a sexual response to breast-feeding a child which fills them with shame and guilt. It follows that a woman may become frigid after childbirth if she has difficulty in integrating adult sexual pleasurable response with maternal bodily response, and marital friction may ensue' (1986, p. 5). However, in my own clinical work what some women are seen to experience with their babies, far from shame and guilt, is such bliss that they do not want to spoil it with anything which might compete for their bodies.

But this does not happen with many other women who are in a similar predicament of becoming pregnant while working as prostitutes. Their depression and sense of unworthiness is such that they feel undeserving of gratification, either in pregnancy or in their relationships with their infants. It is then that those feelings of unworthiness become clearly manifest as a result of an identification with a 'bad' and persecutory mother, as in the following clinical history.

A patient referred herself for psychotherapy because of intense depression. She had made many suicide attempts: 'nothing was worth living for'. She was still working as a prostitute but, according to her own statement, her seeking help had 'nothing to do with it'. She was a forty-six-year-old woman with the most deprived emotional and social background, having had to take care of her mother from the early age of eight, when her father had suddenly died. Before that she had witnessed many violent rows when her father came home completely drunk and beat her mother up. Her mother used to say: 'If only I had had a son he could take care of me.' My patient was the only child, and was regarded as 'scum'. Not only had she never felt wanted, but she saw herself as a heavy burden to her parents. At the age of thirteen she was sent to work, since she had to make a living for both her mother and herself. She had an affair with a married man who advised her to go into prostitution. Very soon she got to know one of her clients, who wanted to marry her in order to become her legitimate pimp. Marriage meant she could easily be recognized as 'a proper woman', which she wanted for her mother's sake. She had already felt obliged to become her own mother's

MOTHER,
MADONNA,
WHORE

mother, so symbolically taking care of her husband only meant taking care of another mother; she performed this function very tenderly and caringly. For her mother's sake she invented a second life for herself: although she worked as a prostitute for her husband, to her mother she pretended that she worked in a restaurant every night as a cashier. She even fabricated characters and described them to her mother in the finest detail: a chef, many waiters, and all the regulars at the restaurant. Every morning after a 'real' full night's work with many freakish clients who expected her to perform all sorts of sado-masochistic games, she would come home to her husband and mother, give her earnings to the former and 'entertain' the latter with funny tales about her non-existent work in the restaurant. She was in reality 'serving' customers and 'feeding' them, so the metaphor was not so far from the truth.

This patient approached motherhood with all kinds of misgivings and mixed expectations. She gave birth to a boy whom she treated from the very beginning with the utmost contempt, feeling inadequate in dealing with him and very guilty that she now had what her mother had so much wanted for herself. She could not allow herself to enjoy having this child, but had to treat him badly as an extension of her mother's frustrated expectations. He was the only being close to her with whom she felt able to act out the sadistic behaviour she had been exposed to herself from a mother who had always resented her, a father who had never acknowledged her, and subsequently a parasitical husband who lived off her 'immoral earnings'. The high price she had to pay for her ill-treatment of her son was that ultimately he not only became a drug dealer and a pimp, but also began to blackmail his mother.

It was extremely difficult for this patient to make any sense out of therapy. She was determined to cling to a subservient role and to see herself as a victim; however many interpretations were given in this regard, her capacity for insight remained unchanged. She felt undeserving of the better inner life that psychotherapy could offer her, and gave up treatment in the belief it worked only for 'middle-class' women.

There are other circumstances in which women seek an ostensible reward which in fact disguises, or results in,

124 punishment. That is the case with women who engage in prostitution with such recklessness that they are easily caught.

When such women appear in court on charges of soliciting they feel that the charge in itself will prejudice everyone against them and that nobody will bother to get to know about them, their upbringing, their emotional needs, and personal circumstances. Such is their despondency that, expecting no real understanding, they usually make the law-enforcers collude with their inner persecutory needs in acquiescing to disproportionately heavy sentences. And, indeed, society feels so hostile, not only to their actions but also to their inability to defend themselves, that it is unable to separate their actions from their personalities. Therefore their sentencing carries with it an unconscious recognition of their actions and of their need for punishment, which is not the case for notorious prostitutes.

Offenders have lived all their lives with others telling them what is wrong with them. They are always ready for a moral dissertation, since 'The antisocial tendency is characterized by an element in it which compels the environment to be important', as Winnicott has said; he adds that 'the antisocial tendency implies hope' (1956, p. 309). Although we can recognize that these women's 'illegal' actions are often at least partly a product of their emotional deprivation, and are sometimes engaged in with hopes of a magical outcome, others seem unable to stop telling them how wrong they are.

Such was the case of a woman aged twenty-seven, who looked sixty when I first saw her many years ago. She had been referred for a psychiatric report to the court because of several charges of soliciting in the streets. Her sort of prostitution was a manifestation of the most self-denigrating and depressed attitudes about herself: she was performing fellatio for fifty pence in the park near where she lived. From the social inquiry I learnt that this woman had appeared in court several times on prostitution charges, and that every time she felt depressed she either relapsed into prostitution or ran away. Her living conditions were described as 'appalling'. She had married a man twenty-nine years her senior who had picked her up once from the streets and had promised to take care of her; he was actually a vagrant who saw the chance to make some profits

and to have a companion for his own misery. My patient's 125
mother had her when she was seventeen and she was given away
at birth to her maternal grandmother, to whom she was
devoted. The father was unknown. Her running away from
home and her fondness for her grandmother emerged several
times in the social inquiry.

This woman had had twelve miscarriages and felt undeserving of becoming a mother. Actually she felt that she did not
deserve anything, not even a psychiatric interview. When she
came into my room for her first meeting she seemed very
guarded, suspicious, and insecure. She sat on the edge of the
armchair, was very red in the face, began to sweat profusely,
and showed some shaking in her hands and legs. Her first words
were: 'Look doctor, I won't do it again. I don't want to waste
your time. I'm sure there must be a lot of people with real
problems.' In saying this she showed a toothless mouth and the
physical appearance of an elderly woman. (The self-denigration
which we worked through afterwards was already showing in
her physical appearance.) Again she mumbled something like:
'I'm very ashamed of myself. I won't do it again.' This claim
was obviously made in an attempt to please the interviewer: she
was already complying with the 'law' and expecting condem-
nation, not seeking real understanding but just a little
recognition of her 'unlawful' actions.

I would like to pursue further this important general
characteristic which appears in female offenders, and to give
special consideration to the inner world of women who have at
some time in their lives practised prostitution. As prostitutes
women are unable to see themselves as separate beings, let
alone as sexual beings. Their self-esteem is very low, they feel
depressed, and they use as defensive mechanisms projection and
splitting. The strong feeling of contempt they show towards
society ('I don't care a damn about them') covers up a massive
projection of their own self-neglect. After all, they are the ones
who are ostracized, despised, isolated, and eventually detained.
They tend to view the external world as something imposed on
them, because they are so much in need of a strong response
from the outside. However negative or severe this response
could be, it provides them in their daily lives with the

narcissistic support which they are unable to obtain from within.

Most professions, regardless of how demanding they can be of our time, emotional involvement, and physical powers, still leave us able to pursue separate public and private lives. In the intimacy of the latter we replenish our mental and physical resources. This is not possible for women who practise prostitution; indeed, the opposite is the case. This aspect of their predicament becomes obvious when they appear in court, where their private lives are exposed to the public. Since their profession involves them in offering and providing their clients with gratifications of a very intimate nature, their own private needs have to be ignored. Everything private becomes public, this being the nature of the conflict. Some women unconsciously hope that, once their problems are acknowledged and in the open, help will become available to them, though usually it does not.

Grunberger portrays narcissism as an autonomous drive with two components, a 'hedonistic' self-love and a 'lethal' component, 'which can evolve in psychic or psychosomatic changes and could end up, in serious cases, in death'. He refuses to identify this 'lethal' component with masochism, since he sees masochism as a relatively advanced mode of object-relations, and therefore contrasted with narcissism. He sees the 'lethal' component as endowed with characteristics of 'object mastery, aggression, omnipotence' (1979, p. 71n.). I believe that women who have engaged in acts of prostitution are seeking not the 'hedonistic', but the 'lethal' component of narcissism. Certainly they do not attempt to create object-relations, for there are none in their professional world. As Aulagnier (1966) has reminded us, in perversion there is a devaluation of narcissistic pleasure: the more it appears linked to dirt, decadence, pain and ignominy, the more it is worn like a crown of martydom, the reversal of narcissism. According to her, 'the perverse woman who has "gone too far" in the erotic game will be likely to say that she did so "in order to give pleasure", presenting her pleasure is a sort of holocaust, a sacrifice offered to the god of pleasure' (p. 75, my translation).

Those who run brothels or similar establishments seem to

'know' the complexities of this narcissistic devaluation pretty well, and do not fail to keep telling the 'girls' how special and unique they are. They even make them compete with one another to see how many 'punters' they are able to book for the night. This is a trap these women find impossible to resist. It is then that they feel 'alive', excited, and full of vigour. Consequently the proprietor's business thrives, but the women subsequently feel like fools, as they will admit afterwards. Everything is back to what it was before, if not worse: even the money they earn has by now lost its financial value and is thrown away, sometimes in a literal sense.

Throughout my clinical practice I have heard women in all walks of life relate fantasies about prostitution. I have examined women who came reluctantly for psychiatric diagnostic reports after having been charged with soliciting. I have treated women who have come of their own volition for psychotherapy and who have been practising prostitutes at some time in their lives. Others have come while still 'working'. But they all had one thing in common: they felt prevented from sharing their intimate lives with their clients. For example, they could not reveal how depressed they were at the thought of ageing, since it is the nature of the trade to offer cheerfulness and youth.

Many times I have heard from middle-aged women who practise prostitution that they are forced to disguise signs of ageing since this would automatically spoil their source of income. (It is more difficult to acknowledge the other hurts.) A patient of mine aged forty-two said: 'I'll have to give the game up, otherwise I'll have to go into kinky activities, since I'm seen as an old bag.' So that is what is left for women who pursue this profession when they reach middle age, just when they need more reassurance than ever about themselves. The biological clock is once more working at maximum speed.

Psychoanalysts often wonder whether sexual perversions exist in females. So why is it that prostitution is a much more frequent phenomenon in women than in men? I believe that the answer is that female prostitution can be seen as a female perversion. I would say that most of the patients I have seen who have worked as prostitutes experience a tremendous sense

THE SYMBOLIC
MOTHER AS
A WHORE

of emptiness. When this becomes unbearable and they feel depressed they turn to prostitution, from which they derive a sense of elation which increases their self-esteem — though this feeling is short-lived, since it is feeding a 'false self' and is immediately replaced by a sense of futility and abandonment.

Some women in prostitution follow a selective and perverse path, one taken also by some men. It resembles the traditional definition of perversion in which intimate relationships are caricatured. The woman has some perverse designs in her mind, which involve varied symbolic operations. She is bitter, assertive and ready for revenge. This revenge, which appears on the surface to be directed against socio-economic submission and against a man's world, is actually directed against her mother. Her desire for revenge is at the same time a desire to be in charge, to have conscious control, and an unconscious denigration of herself and her gender. Like a perverse male individual, she feels elated while with her client; depression and despair soon follow. This is an unconscious process in which she uses denial, splitting, depersonalization and derealization to avoid the experience of psychic pain. The woman feels debased and too depressed to harbour vengeful fantasies against men, as is usually stated. What she really feels is contempt for herself and for her gender, and it is then that she identifies with her male client.

I T IS NOT UNUSUAL to find in women who have practised prostitution in adolescence and adulthood an early history of incest. Of course this is not to say that all victims of incest become prostitutes, or vice versa, but prostitution, as many authors have indicated, is a frequent sequel in cases of father–daughter incest.

As the Ciba Foundation (1984) reports, most clinical studies show that the main long-term effects from which incest victims suffer are promiscuity and sexual coldness, together with an inability to form lasting emotional and sexual relationships. I shall leave aside the group with 'no ill effects', which the nature of my work makes rather inaccessible to me. However, it seems that girls who were incest victims and did not suffer from serious effects have not been blamed and have unconditional support from friends and family members during childhood, an important factor not to be forgotten and one which is very much associated with social and cultural conditions.

It is my suggestion that girls who have been victims of incest see very few alternatives to prostitution upon reaching adulthood. In any event, their bodies will respond in a massive way, either with an exaggeration of the libido or with completely repressed sexuality. Their severe problems range from prostitution to chronic psychosomatic symptoms. In my work over twenty years I have observed acute psychopathology, but have not encountered more positive outcomes such as the absence of sexual or emotional conflicts arising in adulthood in incest survivors.

The two damaging effects, promiscuity and sexual coldness, might seem to be complete opposites, but there are strong connections: I have often encountered women who are promiscuous, or have been involved in promiscuity, whose problems are related to sexual coldness. More often than not promiscuity is accompanied by frigidity, and prostitution by sexual coldness which leads to promiscuous behaviour and perverse sexual fantasies.

Let's start with the 'prostitution solution'. The disparity in statistics reveals a confused picture, but one which corresponds to the nature of the problem — the secrecy surrounding incest. Sloane and Karpinski (1942) found that one out of three female incest victims they studied subsequently became a prostitute. Gagnon (1965) found that 80% of the women he studied had serious sexual problems, including prostitution. Lukianowicz (1972) found that 15% of the incest victims he studied became prostitutes. Goodwin quotes: 'in studies of prostitutes it has been reported that 59% are incest victims' (1982, p. 4); Peters (1976) is another researcher who mentions prostitution as a sequel to incest. Justice and Justice include prostitution as a possible outcome in the adult lives of incest victims, and they add: 'Being a prostitute is consistent with how these women see themselves: tainted, bad, good only for delivering sex' (1979, p. 188). They remind us of a survey conducted in Seattle of two hundred prostitutes, 20% of whom had been incestuously assaulted as children, and also of the Chicago Vice Commission report which had similar findings — 51 of the 103 women questioned said their first sexual experience had been with their own fathers. Silbert and Pines (1981), in their study of two hundred juvenile and adult street prostitutes, found high levels of sexual child abuse in their backgrounds: 70% of the women they studied reported that early sexual abuse was a strong motivation to become prostitutes. Renshaw (1982) found that for some women who practise prostitution there was an early history of sexual contact with a member of the family. These figures are so at variance (20%, 50%, 70%) that surely they are either questionable, or reflect the difficulties of obtaining accurate figures.

In the dynamic process of incest, girls have learnt how to keep to themselves important and intimate secrets. This knowledge is turned into primitive defence mechanisms such as splitting and denial. As Okell Jones and Bentovim (1984) have indicated, 'Children who have been sexually abused often display seductive or sexually provocative behaviour; it is the only way they know of getting attention and is undoubtedly the secondary outcome of being taught that sexual behaviour is what is expected' (p. 6). Their 'knowing it all' and their tendency to self-sacrifice, flamboyancy, and self-destructiveness could be bitterly exploited in adulthood for the 'excellence' of this 'new trade'. It is well known that most incest survivors 'may attract later on in life sexually aggressive and demanding partners' (Ciba Foundation, 1984, p. 16). Are those early acquired 'skills' determining their fate?

Bentovim (1977) has produced an extensive and invaluable study which has highlighted the importance of the family dysfunction in the understanding, treatment, and management of the families with histories of incest. Incest is very much a matter of family dynamics.

Such is the power of incest to produce an exaggerated emotional response that we psychotherapists can easily forget our therapeutic stance and begin to take sides. Countertransference can be affected, as our response in these cases is usually complete empathy with the victim and outrage against the perpetrator. Incest is larger than life, and the victims make us feel possessive about them and very special. Indeed, we are, according to incest victims, imbued with all the 'good' qualities which will enable us to understand them better than anyone else. If we believe this, we are already repeating the emotional characteristics of the incest situation. This 'belief' could make us collude with either the perpetrator or incest victim. We tend to be so much more sympathetic towards the victims than to the perpetrators that it is easy to forget or to ignore the fact that the perpetrators may well have been victims at an earlier stage in their lives. This prejudiced view leaves us in a biased position, unable to comprehend the phenomenon completely. Thus the victim may have our sympathy but she is left without an accurate assessment of her situation, since what happened to her in reality corresponded partly to her own unconscious fantasies. Let us apply the medical model and treat the entire family as the patient, otherwise we may easily become silent conspirators in a system in which only victims are heard. Such a situation could produce undesirable outcomes for everyone concerned, including the abused child.

The importance of family dynamics in incest can hardly be overstressed. Nevertheless, it is not always recognized. Professional workers, especially in the past, have often made incredulous or sceptical remarks about a mother's denial of any knowledge that paternal incest had occurred. Such attitudes are not conducive to accurate diagnosis of the family dynamics. The mother in these cases cannot acknowledge the incest because temporarily she is emotionally and/or physically unable to respond to the demands placed on her as a mother, caretaker, wife, and partner. She is too depressed, detached, or exhausted to accept and fulfil her 'duties'. She can no longer cope. Bitter comments are made about mothers who knew, but didn't know. Some disbelieve their daughters; others ill-treat them when confronted with the reality. At other times, when mother is on the threshold between not knowing and knowing (something like a twilight zone) she is able to hear and acknowledge what is going on, and then she may call upon outside help, from general practitioners, social services, the law, the police. But there must be many cases which remain secret.

Sometimes the 'secret' of incest has been hidden away for years and years. When patients involved in incest situations are very cautious in making critical remarks about their parents or early life history ('Everything was just normal, absolutely fine'), their statements should not necessarily be taken as true. If we listen carefully for what has been omitted from their own histories, incidents usually emerge which point to an early

In other cases, when there is an apparent lack of memory about early childhood events in people who have committed or have been involved in sexual offences, it may be fruitful to investigate further to see whether they have blocked off episodes from early childhood which are too painful to recall. This could be particularly relevant for the incest victim's mother, who not infrequently turns out to have been an incest victim herself.

Sometimes the daughter unconsciously colludes in the incest, not only because of her father's demands but also because she is responding to her mother's inability to cope. That is why most girls report their fathers' sexual assaults on them only when the father takes another daughter for this 'duty'. The first girl then feels debased and betrayed, not so much because her position as her father's favourite is being usurped but because she is no longer the one chosen to fulfil this 'duty' for her mother. Before the incest, she felt her mother did not understand her and she longed to get closer to her. Sometimes, she has even become her own mother's mother in an effort to create some sense of intimacy with her. So incest, if this is required, seems inevitable.

I repeat that secrecy, especially in paternal incest, is at the core of the situation: each member of the family is involved, whether 'knowing' or 'unknowing', but nobody talks about it. Indeed, it is irrelevant when paternal incest has occurred whether mother acknowledges the possibility of incest or not; had she been able to acknowledge it in the first place, incest would never have happened. Incest is committed in an effort to create ties to 'keep the family together'. Secrecy is the new taboo which has emerged from the breakdown of the taboo against incest (Ciba Foundation, 1984, p. 13). Nobody 'knows' about it, or rather nobody acknowledges it.

I have seen some female patients with a history of early incest who, when entering group analytical therapy, behave from the very start as 'ideal assistants' to the therapist. Even those who had previously never been familiar with the unconscious processes seem to discover immediately appro-priate ways to 'help' the therapist/mother/father keep the

134 group/family together. Fellow patients often react with surprise and bewilderment, and later with competitiveness. When interpretations are made to the effect that the newcomer is repeating a pathological pattern learnt early in life, fellow patients seem relieved by this understanding but it is then the turn for the newcomer to be filled with rage at this interpretation. After all, 'she is doing her best'; why is she being so 'harshly criticized'?

Is prostitution also a symbolic manoeuvre to keep a family together? Does the function of prostitution preserve the family by means of an outside 'sex provider' when things do not seem to work at home or when there are strains that need to be relieved by an outside agency? Are incest victims better able than others to deal with the professional hazards of prostitution in later life? In this light incest could almost be considered a sort of apprenticeship. This has been simply stated by Herman: '. . . the father, in effect, forces the daughter to pay with her body for affection and care which should be freely given. In so doing he destroys the protective bond between parent and child and initiates his daughter into prostitution' (1981, p. 4). Herman also expands on the feelings of power over others that these women experience as 'guardians of the incest secret'. The girls' fantasies are often confirmed by their fathers who tell them in a threatening way that they are able either to destroy their families or keep them together. Herman notes that in the course of prostitution these women learnt, some by mere chance, that among men who pursue prostitutes are those who are easily 'turned on' by accounts of incest (p. 98).

The evolution of an incest situation goes through many stages. Typically it begins with a masked breakdown of the family structure, which perhaps is not consciously felt by any of its members. There may be, or appear to be, some specific events which, when they come to light later on, are identified as 'causes' of incest. For example, very often the process begins with the wife refusing to have sex with her husband. This makes the husband feel insecure and inadequate, and leads to the distress and marked regression which is characteristic of the incest perpetrator. When he feels unwanted by his wife he seeks in his daughters or sons not simply sexual gratification, but also warmth and reassurance. These men react in such an exaggerated way because this new situation often brings nightmarish echoes from their own childhood in which similar cumulative traumas occurred. Once more we have to use the three-generational approach, its dynamics, and its links to socio-economic and cultural factors if we are to understand the actions of each and every member of the family.

I have heard from many male patients who have committed incest how much they have felt rejected by their wives, and also been made to feel small, humiliated and inadequate just as they did when they were young children with a very possessive, domineering, or neglectful mother. A period of impotence towards their wife can be a clinical indication that the incest is about to begin. In quite a number of cases this relates to the wife's new pregnancy and labour, or depression. The patient usually talks about his wife's coolness, distancing, and frigidity, and describes her as not wanting to have sex with him. He feels unable to pursue any extramarital affairs, indeed he claims he has never dreamt of being unfaithful to his wife. He even talks about incest as 'keeping sex in the family' (to him this seems to be less of a betrayal of his wife than were he to go outside the family), and there is no cynicism attached to this statement. The 'solution' in these cases, especially for a couple in which there is some emotional deprivation and lack of communication, seems to be the seduction of a child.

I remember a male patient who had maintained sexual relationships with his stepdaughter for five years, starting when the girl was six. His attraction towards her started when his wife became pregnant and refused to have sex with him. He felt able to contain his sexual urges, to wait until after the baby's birth and the readjustment of the family situation. A few months later when the baby died a cot death, his wife became deeply depressed and unable to meet his sexual requirements. The baby's short life had been a very stormy period, with daily fights between the parents. After the baby's death the husband withdrew, but was unable to express any feelings of grief. Instead, he suddenly felt prompted from within to approach his stepdaughter sexually. He did not know why he did it, except that he was in great need of warmth, care,

SUBSTITUTE
MOTHERHOOD

and human contact. In his own words: 'It occurred to me that it might be preferable to approach my girl since she is part of the family and very much part of myself.' During treatment he became aware of his intense anger, his own very low sense of self-esteem, and his wish for revenge against his wife as represented by her daughter. The situation had been complicated by the fact that he had secretly accused his wife of the baby's death, which happened one night when he was away from home after a fight. He was projecting his own guilt on to his wife, since in his view the baby would not have died had he been there. He also observed his own inability to mourn his child, and his manic defence in abusing the child who had survived.

Incest operates on a number of different levels simultaneously in different family members: (1) A discharge of tension between husband and wife. (2) Satisfaction and sexual gratification where the object, or actually part-object, is easily available and can be seduced, always in a very secretive manner. (3) This secrecy which, it must be stressed, is the key to understanding incest, because it includes a degree of special recognition and favour within the family situation for that particular child . . . (These three characteristics appear very vividly in the transference, not only in the course of treatment but also during the first interview, meeting, or diagnostic session.) (4) A discharge of intense hostility: revenge directed towards the wife in the person of 'her child'. (5) Re-establishment of some sort of family dynamics or balance. (6) Disclosure of the secret after a certain point, when incest is no longer necessary to the family dynamics.

It is very important to notice the family circumstances when the facts are disclosed. Is the wife over her depression, or her mourning period? Is she able to be 'present' now? Has she resumed sexual intercourse with her husband? Or has another daughter become aware that her sister is the 'favourite one' and so felt undermined? Is this the moment at which another sibling suffering from intense jealousy towards the incest victim denounces father and sister?

MOTHER,
MADONNA,
WHORE

Let me share with you some of the predicaments my patients have entrusted me with, and the few means of escape they contrive for their survival. The degree of intensity of the trauma and the age at which they were abused determine their subsequent level of self-esteem, and accordingly the quality of life they feel they deserve.

An intelligent, divorced woman of thirty-five was referred by her GP (family doctor) for psychiatric diagnosis on account of her susceptibility to becoming involved in violent relationships with men. A fixed pattern had been established in which she always chose boyfriends who had a violent nature, and she encouraged this violence in them by striking the first blow. The outcome was always the same — she ended up covered with bruises, for which she frequently consulted her GP. She also helped her lovers to manipulate her physically and mentally, though this only took place when she felt emotionally close to them. She had had three children, by three different men with whom she had had erratic relationships until they were abruptly terminated by the men, in each case after her pregnancy.

When I saw this patient for the first time she was yearning to enter into individual therapy with a woman. This, I believed, was the manifestation of a deep longing for a union with a responsive and caring mother who valued her own femininity, and was also able to put up with her hate and revenge towards her own mother. She feared that a man could easily be manipulated and seduced by her, since in a way she unconsciously 'knew' this would be her fantasized outcome, for her to feel so powerfully seductive but simultaneously deprived of any 'real' help. It had taken her a long time and many painful experiences to come to the conclusion that she had to 'risk' trusting a woman.

She mentioned casually that prostitution 'was my profession' and that in this field she had always felt safe from any emotional or physical problems. For instance, she had never encountered any violent attacks during the course of her work, nor had she felt emotionally involved with any of her clients. Her own speciality was sadomasochism, in which her clients would ask her to play out with them masochistic games in which they were subject to her physical punishment and denigration.

138   She regarded her work not only as the source of a good income, but also as providing her with the freedom to choose her own working hours 'during school time', leaving her adequate free time to spend with her three children, whose company she very much enjoyed. The oldest child, a boy, when he got to know about her prostitution, said, according to her, 'It's better to keep quiet about it. If it brings money who cares?'

The extreme 'splitting' that characterized her daily life was only too obvious. Her relationships functioned on two totally separate levels and with two completely different sets of needs. This splitting was an asset to her in her successful pursuit of her profession. In her work she was self-assured and assertive, but also sadistic; her need for revenge was alive here. But she was completely cut off from her other needs and fears, and there was no real involvement on her side. On the other hand, in her emotional relationships she felt anxious and inadequate, and she was very self-critical. She was preoccupied with herself, to the point of self-obsession, and with the needs that arose from her extreme dependency and fear of being left alone. She showed a most masochistic nature.

You might well wonder now what her early life was like. Her mother had left home when the child was only eleven months old. Her first memories were of her father blaming her for her mother's departure from home. She had always felt humiliated, denigrated, and abandoned because of being a girl. Who knows what had happened to her mother around the time of her own birth which may have prompted her to leave home soon after a daughter arrived? When my patient reached the age of four a male relative sexually assaulted her. She felt extreme pain, and was utterly confused and unable to make any sense of what was happening. She broke down and in tears managed to tell her father about it. His angry — and by his own standards, 'justifiable' — response was to start an incestuous relationship with her which lasted for many years. After all, if she had been held responsible for mother's absence, why not cast her as mother's replacement? This was to be the start of many other incestuous situations, since whatever male in the family she approached about her predicament, he too was to join the list of her sexual abusers.

Despite this, when in need of help she had until now approached only men. Her complete lack of trust in women had to do with the way she had experienced her own mother leaving her. Her father, on the other hand, had not only stayed with her, but had also taken care of her. Even in the incest she felt that there was some quality of involvement, and she had been made to feel very special to him, though she was not at all able to control the situation. So why not approach men rather than women about her problems? She 'knew' that, at the very least, she could get a physical response if not an emotional one. She had never got either from her mother. But the high price which she had to pay for survival was a complete division of her emotional and physical needs and gratifications from normal life. It was only too consistent with her life history that prostitution seemed a suitable solution. After all, nobody had been very concerned with her emotions when she was an infant. Her body had been the only successful vehicle through which to convey or to elicit any emotions or sensations.

This woman found prostitution to be the solution, not only because it relieved her of the intense pain, depression, hopelessness, and impotence she had gone through so very early in life, but also because it provided her with a means to gain revenge for those traumatic and damaging experiences. Now, as opposed to before, she felt in complete control, and was herself the perpetrator of humiliations. She viewed her work in utilitarian terms: 'only two days in the week and it's never bothered me'. Again, in her own words: 'It was only five years ago that I realized I was not here in the world for men's pleasure, but for myself.'

Paradoxically, this woman experienced prostitution as her one and only way to do something for herself and not for men. But her self-betrayal was evident in her emotional relationships, in which she was punished terribly for what her 'other half' was doing.

In psychoanalytical terms you could say that her superego, however erratic, was as in many perversions still functioning in the most implacable manner. It kept on punishing her for her extremely guilty feelings. Where did this guilt come from? It may have had to do with her own incestuous fantasies about her father; perhaps it was linked to an enormous distaste for herself and her body, present since her arrival in the world, when her birth was not at all welcomed because she was a girl and therefore more easily available for her father's incest.

Are we then really talking in terms of a social, generalized guilt, one which can create such a powerful superego? It had taken her a long time to ask for help, even if it was not directly related to her prostitution, which she actually felt to be ego-syntonic (in other words, compatible with her ego's integrity) because of her early experiences. I believe that age is an important factor. This woman was thirty-five: she had had enough of it. The 'as if' personality with its secondary gains was fading away, and she now felt ready to embark on an exploratory voyage which might lead her to the realization of her true self.

Another patient was referred by her probation officer on account of 'her depression, her very unsatisfactory relationships, and her work as a prostitute'. She was half an hour late for her appointment, already an indication of her mixed feelings about consulting a psychiatrist, though she was able to admit to this and also to the uncertainty she experienced about her own motivations for being sent to me. She had been in conflict with the law for soliciting over the previous six years; she had been the subject of probation orders and had received custodial sentences of eighteen, six and three months. She also remarked that her present three-year probation order was coming to an end and that she was faced with another court appearance because she had been caught soliciting after a long period of being 'clear'. There is often a relapse into new troubles with the law when the sense of containment which is provided by a probation order is removed. The new acting-out is an unconscious substitute for more outside control.

My patient had a most traumatic and deprived background. Her mother died when she was two months old. Her father tried to have her fostered, but this did not occur until she was five years old. Until then she lived with her father, his second wife and later on two half-brothers. She remembered being ill-treated by her stepmother, and things did not improve at all with her new adoptive family: she was again physically punished. She quite liked going to school, because it took her away from home, and she did six 'O' levels. She used to run away from home frequently. On one of these escapades, when she was thirteen years old, she contacted her real father hoping for support and reassurance. She did not get it. Her father drove her in his car to a nearby park and attempted to have sexual intercourse with her. She protested vehemently and, in order to get away, told him that she was menstruating. He then forced her to perform fellatio on him under the threat of beating her up and of telling her adoptive parents of her bitter complaints about them. She still vividly remembered how terrified and disgusted she was. She went back to her foster-parents feeling utterly despondent. At seventeen she met a boy of the same age and got pregnant. He was very reluctant to take any responsibility to start with, and wanted her to have an abortion. She insisted on having the baby, and he married her after their daughter was born. During their short marriage she was constantly humiliated and physically punished by him. A separation took place. After that she met a man who suggested she took up prostitution, and she began to go to Park Lane every night with other girls also 'on the game'. She used to make around £500 a night, all of which went into the pocket of this man, with whom she was living. Sometimes she would go to her clients' places, and sometimes to her own place, where her partner in the next room would force her to extract more and more money from her clients.

It was very painful to my patient when her former husband won custody of their daughter, but she was unable to contest it. When the girl was about four years old, she went to the school and took her daughter away. She kept her daughter for almost a year, but then her partner made her give her daughter up since this arrangement seriously affected her capacity to make money. From then on she began to take overdoses, and was taken to hospital more than once, until her partner decided to leave her. Three months before my interview with her she had had to spend two days in gaol, and then was released on bail through the intervention of her probation officer, with whom she got on very well. After that she decided to apply for a job in order to be considered fit to have access to her daughter.

142   Eventually she was allowed, under close supervision, to see her daughter once a fortnight, but these were difficult visits, leaving mother resentful and daughter confused. She then opted out and never saw her daughter again, in the belief that 'this would be better for the two of us'.

Mrs G, a woman of thirty-five, referred herself for treatment by letter on account of having 'reached desperation point with a psychosexual problem'. When she first came to see me she appeared as a charming, bright woman, open about her problems, with a capacity for insight and motivation for treatment.

She was an accomplished and very successful scholar, and said that nobody who knew her in her professional life would ever dream of her being in need of psychiatric help, such was the picture of self-containment and contentment she showed to the outside world. Her inner world was another matter. She said she 'had had enough of hopping around in bed with new guys' and admitted to feelings of despair, hopelessness, and general misery.

Some years ago, after her divorce, she had taken up part-time prostitution as an attempt to solve her inner conflicts 'intellectually', without having to appeal for professional help or 'wasting her friends' and acquaintances' time or giving them cause for embarrassment' with her 'ridiculous problems'. After looking through some of the relevant publications she made contacts which allowed her to develop her problems into 'skills' and 'advantages' to be used in her new part-time occupation. During that period of her life she was in control of all her 'newly acquired relationships' in such a way that she soon became uninterested and bored with it all, since everyone who paid for her services did exactly what she demanded of them. Stoller remarks on this very same phenomenon when he describes a prostitute talking about mystery and boredom after a year in the trade: 'The wrong kind of excitement, that which threatens to reveal its origins, withers excitement' (1975, p. 107). My patient would excite her clients by offering everything but giving very little of herself; this, she said, thrilled them. She would 'torture them without pity', letting them see bits of her body, and eventually allowing them 'to touch her a little'. This display was accompanied by her ordering them about. The more she did so, the more excited the men became. It was obvious that she had become an expert in the sadomasochistic speciality of prostitution. After a while she gave it all up, even though she got her 'mystery' and an enormous sense of satisfaction from wondering what her colleagues would have made out of her 'extramural' activity.

She told me of a pattern which had evolved in her life over the past eighteen years. She would meet a man and fall for him and find him sexually extremely attractive, and they would start sexual activities in which she was very much the teacher. She found this exciting, but around three or four months later something seemed suddenly to switch off. What she had at first found so gratifying and elating would now become the object of her contempt and disgust. Then she would find it terrifying to have men close to her, even to the extent of becoming phobic, and she would abruptly end the affair. Immediately afterwards she would proceed to get involved in a new relationship which developed in the same way. She felt distressed and wanted to be able to maintain a steady relationship.

This pattern was established after her search for her estranged father succeeded. The problem was not only that she met her father at the age of seventeen for the first time in her life, but that in their first meeting he was only too obvious in his sexual approach to her. She said she wanted so much to be close to him, and was shocked that while she wanted affection, she received instead a sexual response. After the initial blunder she gave in, since both of them wanted very badly to have sexual intercourse. Despite the fact that this happened on many occasions, her father was always impotent with her. She felt deeply frustrated about his non-performance. When she began to make links between her present predicament and her experiences with her father she decided not to see her father again, and she became aware of her need for professional help.

Her birth was due to an accident: 'just the result of fucking on the lawn between two people in between two marriages'. Her mother was twenty, had never wanted to have children, and tried to abort her without success. As a young girl she was told that after her birth her mother had tried to strangle her. According to my patient, her mother was obsessed with sex, promiscuous, not at all interested in emotional involvements but concerned only about the erotic pleasures she could obtain from her body. She separated from her husband as soon as my patient was born and sent her to be brought up with her own mother, who was very strict and puritanical and never allowed mother and daughter to get together. She was sent to a Catholic convent.

Mrs G had no early recollection, and I assume that there was very little for her to remember which was pleasant or caring. However she remembered her grandmother's death when she was fifteen, since she then decided to harden herself and not to experience any grief. She became close to her mother, who showed an obsessive preoccupation with her adolescent daughter's body and sexual education. This was done in a rather perverse way, pushing and encouraging her to get involved in sex, but advising her to do so with only very experienced and skilful men.

Mrs G considered in hindsight that this had not been wise since she began a series of associations with 'macho' men and their male friends, who were technically experienced but lacked any tenderness or care. Her mother was so involved with her daughter's sexuality that she could not wait for her to come home, when she would demand detailed descriptions of her daughter's sexual experiences. Eventually my patient got pregnant and had a back-street abortion, which was very traumatic.

It was at this point, when she was completely disillusioned with her mother, that she decided to turn to her unknown father for some recognition, and there began the ordeal already described. Her academic achievements were her only source of gratification and self-value. Even this began to wear thin as the years went by; the split between affect and intellect had gone too far for her to sustain it any longer. She felt on the verge of being uncontained and sensed the imminence of a complete breakdown of her precariously maintained defences.

Yet another patient, Mrs M, aged twenty-five, was referred for treatment by a general hospital because of her difficulties in relationships and her frigidity, following a four-year period working as a 'high-class' prostitute. When I first saw her I was struck by her physical appearance of naïvety, virginity, and purity; she looked the epitome of the 'English Rose'. I was also impressed by her firm determination to get help for her problems. However, she had let two years elapse since breaking away from 'the game' before she felt entitled to claim a genuine need for herself. In her own words:

I decided to give it all up because the price I had to pay for the money I was making was excessive. That lifestyle transformed sex into an ugly and rotten thing which had nothing to do with love or intimacy . . . I began to see men at their worst, and I considered them to be just like animals, but very fast I learnt how to switch off my feelings, and began to experience myself as if there were two different persons inhabiting me. I never saw the daylight, since I lived only by night. I was unable to make any friends because I was full of shame, but on the other hand I was made to feel very important because in the nightclubs where I worked as a 'hostess' everyone was considered to be extremely special. Soon afterwards I realized this had to do with scoring against other hostesses, how many screws we were asked for, and how much we charged. So we were just objects to be used. I began to feel utterly depressed and drank a lot. Money was important in the making, but as soon as I got it I would throw it away, even on the platform at Paddington Station, and I was never able to buy anything nice for myself. Money was just a symbol of what I was worth in the eyes of others. I thought, 'Shit, I'm getting a raw deal, I want out of this'.

Then she proceeded to tell me how carefully she had thought about what sort of work she would be fit to do. Firstly, she decided against any night-time occupation, she had had enough of it. But what about people? She had had more than enough of them too. So she dismissed the idea of working in close association with either men or women: men, because she had seen their 'animal' characteristics; women, because she had suffered through their competitiveness and false feelings of being so special, 'all very deceptive'. What was left for her? She was a young, articulate, intelligent woman who felt that she owed her life to others, and wanted to make things better for everyone around. I must say, I was impressed by her professional choice. She loved growing things, so she became a florist — 'flowers are beautiful and they make you feel good by arranging them in particular ways'. She had become a prestigious professional in the field, and it was then that she sought psychotherapy.

Mrs M had a disturbed background. She was the ninth in a family of thirteen, and at the age of eight she was sent together with an older brother to live with a maternal uncle and his wife. She was told that this was because her parents were poor and could not cope with all the children's demands, but could not understand why she and her brother were 'the chosen ones' for this removal from their home. However, the new home was much better, and at first she was able to adjust quite well to the change. But problems soon began. Her old and ailing uncle began to make tentative physical approaches to her. At the start she felt inadequate in dealing with them, since she had been told by her mother that she should feel grateful to her uncle and aunt for welcoming her into their home. Presently, she was the object of her uncle's sexual provocation, and in no time she was fulfilling a mistress's task. She was revolted by it all, but was still unable to reject her uncle because she felt it was 'her duty' to go along with his requests. When she was sixteen her uncle developed osteo-rheumatoid arthritis, and she had to give up school to look after him. Her aunt told her that that was the price she had to pay for having been brought up by them. She made some rebellious moves but desisted when her uncle, on account of his illness, tried to commit suicide. When he died, her aunt kicked her out and she went to work as a nanny for a married couple with a young child. In no time she had an affair with the man. Both wife and husband tried to make this work as a threesome, but it didn't so she left for London. Here she fell into the nightclub scene and the world of prostitution.

The case of this woman is quite remarkable. I was impressed with her from the very beginning, and I knew she would do well since she had been able to achieve a lot on her own before she approached anyone for help. She had fought her way out of the brothels and rejected the pimps. Clearly her early life, at least until the age of eight, had been secure and solid, even if economically precarious. This was an important reassurance in her later life and provided her with some self-assertiveness for survival in her predicament. But as soon as she left the home where she had felt herself to be the victim of abuse, she turned towards revenge and self-destruction.

The 'prostitution solution' is a repetition of earlier traumas in which the survivor tries without success to sort out her life but fails to do so, because she feels imprisoned in the old, familial or familiar pattern, and yet again exploited.

As I have mentioned, another possible outcome in adult life of incest is a total repression of sexuality associated with severe psychosomatic symptoms. This is usually diagnosed as a 'neurotic' disturbance. However, sometimes the damage such sufferers inflict on their bodies and minds is such that it has made me wonder if there are not underlying perverse aspects to their 'neurotic' problems, especially in view of the intrinsic conflicts to do with female sexuality and the way these women abuse their bodies. This would be especially so when sadism, beginning as an expression of revenge against parental figures, is later generalized to everyone who dares to get close.

Such was the case with a patient I saw some years ago, who was urgently referred by her GP. He telephoned in great alarm about a forty-two-year-old woman who had been his patient for twenty years with severe psychosomatic complaints. These ranged from asthma, palpitations, headaches, migraines, and sharp pains in the chest to disorders of the digestive tract. When no solution was found she began to beg for surgical operations to relieve her of excruciating pains. She had never been able to feel close to anyone.

The GP was a caring practitioner, well-informed on psychosomatic disorders, who found himself in the hopeless situation of not being able to understand what was wrong with his patient, of refusing to collude in her schemes of self-mutilation, and of being unable to help her. He described her as a sensitive, pleasant, intelligent, undemanding woman, and not at all 'hysterical'. She lived in complete social isolation and was a successful academic, had never had any relationships with either sex, and appeared to be self-contained and stable except for her physical condition which would at times, render her unable to fulfil her duties. She never got any secondary gains from her symptoms (unless you could so describe a complete inability to establish any intimate relationship).

Suddenly, after all those years of hopelessness and helplessness, she appeared one day in a state of complete emotional distraction. She was then able to tell her GP, for the first time in her life, of an incestuous relationship with her father which had begun when she was ten and had continued until she was twenty-two, when she had found strength enough to break it off and leave home. To start with she had complied with her father's demands because she felt terrified and unable to 'disobey' him. These demands began when her mother had a pregnancy following a stillbirth.

In this context, Lewis (1979) makes an important contribution to the discussion of stillbirth followed by a 'quick replacement pregnancy' which prevents these mothers from mourning the lost baby. He considers this to be a hidden predisposing factor towards child abuse. According to his clinical experience, some mothers who find themselves in this particular predicament of not being able to mourn, coupled with the demands of the newly born baby, could abuse the new infant. In the cases he mentions a mother threatened to batter her baby, and another murdered her eldest child eight months after the birth of a baby, her husband having died suddenly during the pregnancy. He adds that the stillbirth can produce family difficulties that lead to violence (p. 327). I wonder if the occurrence of stillbirth could be another predisposing factor for father– or mother–daughter incest in the family dynamics?

To return to the history of my forty-two-year-old patient: she was the eldest daughter and felt very protective towards her mother, longing for an intimate relationship with her which never took place. After breaking off the incestuous situation with her father and leaving home, she promised to herself never ever to remember this again. She successfully complied with this inner mandate for twenty-two years. Her mind had never bothered her again with those terrible memories, but instead her body had started a relentless and exhausting persecution, manufacturing psychosomatic complaints from unconscious motivations to which she did not have access. She had never told anyone of her attacks against her body. She indulged in self-mutilation, with rituals which involved masturbatory practices of the most sadomasochistic nature.

It is my contention that women who fight against their bodies in such a formidable, repetitive, direct, and symbolical manner, including a sadistic element of revenge against their mothers, are displaying perverse manifestations. I am very much aware that in these particular cases there are grounds for preferring the designation 'neurotic' to 'perverse', but again there is much to be gained from attempting to understand how the female superego develops.

As Irigaray has asked: 'For why is the woman's, the hysteric's, superego so "critical", so cruel? Several reasons might be adduced . . .' There is 'one reason that overlaps several others: *whatever works as a superego for women apparently has no love for women, and particularly of women's sex/ organ(s)*' (quoted by Sayers, 1986, pp. 43–4, author's italics).

Any attempt to study the formation of ego-ideal, superego, and mental representations in the development of a woman who as a young girl had a history of incest appears either as a formidable task or a futile pursuit. A typical background includes a withdrawn and depressed mother who was there, but not there, and an insecure, needy, demanding, violent, and sexual father. Not only was the girl deprived of maternal care and consistent love, for which mourning is not considered to be appropriate, but manic defences were used in the family dynamics to cope with the mother's 'absenteeism'. She felt 'forced' by those parental figures to take over her mother's place in the family in order to secure its stability. So, those who were supposed to contribute to the formation of her ego and superego submitted her to a role reversal and made her feel unable to assert herself against those parental pressures. She became her own mother's mother and wife/mistress to her father, with all the inherent harmful implications. Consequently, her ego, ego-ideal, superego, and id are all mixed up and lacking any external or internal frame of reference.

If we look at such a girl's internal world and its mental representations, a chaotic picture emerges. Let us try to make some sense of the formation of those mental mechanisms as described by various authors. For example, when Nunberg (1955) differentiates the ego-ideal from the superego, he says that the ego submits to the ego-ideal out of love and to the superego out of fear of punishment. In other words the ego-ideal is to be formed by identification with love-objects (mother) while the superego is to be formed later by identification with that of dreaded figures (p. 146) — later fear of the father. For the girl victim of incest, it seems to me that her formation of an ego-ideal with a quasi-absent mother is seriously impeded, and simultaneously the dreaded figure of her father, theoretical provider of her superego, erupts into her life and demands from her an identification with her mother's role. No wonder that her formation of an ego-ideal and a superego are extremely distorted and intermeshed with one another, or that fragments of both are present in a most erratic and inconsistent way.

Lagache's description of the ego-ideal responding to the way in which the subject must behave in order to comply with the expectations of authority, and of the superego corresponding to authority (quoted by Laplanche and Pontalis, 1973, p. 145), seems to me particularly relevant to incest, in which girls are so vulnerable to the forces of authority.

According to Reich (1986), the ego-ideal is in direct relation to the regulation of self-esteem and corresponds to a deep longing that the child has to become like the parent, and 'under certain conditions *magic identification* with the glorified parent — megalomaniac feelings — may replace the *wish* to be like him' (p. 303, author's italics). She also mentions that in narcissistic persons (though she is talking just of women) there appears a fantasy of the whole body being a phallus, the paternal phallus, which arises from deep fixations and over-sexualization; all this occurs in the phallic phase.

There is a great gap in these women's stages of development, mostly a generational one, in which there is a role reversal. They have had to function as a mistress, as a mother, and as an adult when they are often prepubescent. Unable to grow emotionally, thay have been forced to grow sexually. It is immensely significant that everything takes place within the family and that the basic boundaries between responsibilities normally defined by the generations are not respected. The normal parents-children relationship is no longer one in which the parents take care of a daughter and allow her to develop at her own pace. At an early age, the girl who is the victim of incest is the mistress of the household, privy to the most intimate secrets of the family.

The clinical histories of my patients relevant to this theme include seduction and emotional deprivation, being seen and treated as part-objects, being prevented from individuating themselves from parental figures, and being prematurely sexualized by their parents. These are similar characteristics to those found not only in the psychogenesis but also in the clinical manifestations of perversion.

These women suffer from a masked depression covered by a compulsive, disguised, genital sexual activity which is motivated by a deep need for revenge. These 'sexual' inter-actions lack intimacy, emotional nurturing, a sense of con-tinuity, and sexual gratification. Instead, they provide only a short-lived period of elation which is soon replaced by a sense of isolation and despair. Successful soliciting produces a manic response, 'a sense of high' which is very short-lived. This system of regulating the self-esteem is doomed to failure since the motivation for physical encounters is based on hatred rather than love, and the objects encountered — whether represented by their own bodies or their clients' — are mere symbolic replacements for the real ones to which they are directing their revenge.

Incest gives much and then takes everything away, all at once. The little girl is now supposed to have all that she could have dreamt of in her wildest unconscious fantasies, including her father as her lover. And what does this situation bring for her? She shares a secret with Daddy that nobody knows about. Her dreams have become true. Now she has Daddy's love, penis, the lot. And she is left in utter misery, with a complete lack of trust in anyone. Those who were supposed to look after her, and to keep firm boundaries between her worlds of fantasy and reality, have failed her, and all is now confusion. She has an enormous sense of loneliness. Such girls have difficulties in acknowledging any angry feelings because these feelings are extremely intense. They feel angry with their mother, who they see as having failed to protect them, and angry with their father because he has abused them. As a patient of mine said, 'I hate women and distrust men.' They have been left with deep scars which will have a marked impact not only on their emotional lives, but also on all their physical relationships since they often feel that the only way to gain love is through sexualization.

This phenomenon is comparable to the one described by Chasseguet-Smirgel in the creation of the future male pervert, in which his mother makes him believe he is 'her perfect partner with his prepubescent penis and there is nothing left to envy his father' (1985a, p. 29). In my view, the girl seduced by her father is also made to believe, by her father, that she is his perfect partner, but instead of the 'prepubescent penis' of the boy counterpart, she responds to her father's seduction with her whole prepubescent body. Everything is there to be developed and to be tuned in; she can now learn how to respond with her whole body, all her erogenous zones, to her father's seduction. She is just like the boy that Chasseguet-Smirgel talks about, left with nothing to envy his father for, except that the prepubescent girl can still envy her mother's fecundity; but this is a transitional stage, and after the menarche she too is capable of becoming fecund. While in the case of the seduced boy there is usually an open conspiracy of mother-boy and denigration of the father, for father-girl incest secrecy is the rule. The generation boundaries have been offended and violated in both cases. And just as the boy will react later on with perverse personality traits, so likewise will girls.

Chasseguet-Smirgel does not compare the two cases as such, because she believes that for the little girl this realization does not have the 'same sense of return to a primitive state of fusion which is only possible through union with the primary object' (1985a, p. 32). However, the girl is doing so through her bodily association with her father. Whereas Chasseguet-Smirgel believes that the generation difference has to be acknowledged by the boy because his mother has a vagina that he cannot satisfy, the girl on the contrary, is left in a position that while she might not be ready for father to impregnate her, she can satisfy her father's sexual desires or demands by offering him her vagina.

Chasseguet-Smirgel admits that the situation of a girl loved too tenderly by father, who ostensibly prefers her to his wife, is often met with. However, she insists that this girl becomes neurotic and not perverse and adds that 'perhaps this is the reason why perversion is less common in women than in men' (1985b, p. 14). She adheres faithfully to Freud's change in his 'seduction theory', that is, that reported cases of sexual abuse by fathers in his female patients were products of their fantasy. But I think that we have enough evidence by now to go back to his early theory of real seduction, which gives us a rudimentary approach to the object-relationship, since the cause of the sexual problem is rooted in a person (Klein, I. M., 1981)

McCarthy clearly and courageously states: 'I think it is a criticism of the contribution of Psychoanalysis to Psychiatry and allied professions that locating the theme of incest in the world of unconscious fantasy deflected attention away from the reality of incest and delayed the discovery of sexual abuse within the family' (1982, p. 11). He notes that very often patients describing incestuous experiences were labelled psychotic or grossly hysterical.

Time and again we observe the disastrous effects of fathers' interfering with their daughters' emotional and sexual development, similar to the effects on a boy of a seductive and incestuous mother. It is to be hoped that the recognition of these problems could lead to their accurate diagnosis.

In this chapter I have described some cases of paternal incest with which I am familiar and which have led some female incest survivors to prostitution, and others to experience a complete suppression of any intimate relationships. Incest survivors of either sex have enormous difficulties in forming relationships. This is consistent with the state of confusion produced by early, traumatic, and abusive experiences. On the one hand, they feel exploited, abused, and treated as part-objects, completely sexualized; on the other hand, they feel superior, omnipotent, precocious, and precious.

154   The defence mechanisms employed in these cases include deep splitting, denial, and depersonalization. The actions of these women are the products of an intense disgust towards their bodies which they try to resolve by different means, not just by prostitution. However, a relentless sadistic attack on their whole bodies is frequently the norm, sometimes with exaggerated libidinal activity and sometimes with its repression. This distinctive behaviour seems to contain perverse traits which are different from male perversions.

EPILOGUE

The foregoing chapters have in a sense written themselves. They arose more or less spontaneously out of the evidence my patients brought to me. This process has left some loose ends. It would be tidy to draw them together and to end the book with a set of conclusions; tidy, but premature. Despite the flood of publications and advances of recent years, we do not fully understand female sexuality and family dynamics. We are still a long way from being able to write the last word on the subject, and I have not tried to do so. I have been more concerned to say what is perhaps the first word on some of the predicaments that happen to have come to my notice. But since novelty can be provocative, even if in some cases it is only a variant of what has been said before, it may be helpful to conclude with a few remarks and to try to put my findings into focus.

Firstly, it is important to remember the point made in Chapter 1: that throughout the book the word 'perversion' has been used to define an accepted clinical entity in which the individual afflicted does not feel free to obtain sexual genital satisfaction, but instead feels subjected to a compulsive activity that takes over and involves unconscious hostility. In this usage it is a technical, psychoanalytical term and carries no moral connotations. I prefer to use 'perversion' rather than 'deviation', since the latter implies only a statistical abnormality.

Secondly, it is obvious but important to recognize that in the main I have been talking about people who have come to me or have been referred to me because they are suffering from very considerable problems. The fact that these problems can be traced to certain specific events or attitudes does not mean that all those who have experienced similar events or attitudes will suffer the same consequences. Thus, for example, not every girl who is the victim of incest will become a prostitute; nor are all prostitutes victims of incest. To put it more generally, the victims of perverse actions or attitudes will not necessarily act in a perverse way themselves. But no one should doubt the extra strain and difficulty of achieving mental equilibrium if perverse parental behaviour has been inflicted in early life.

Morality is unquestionably involved in the way individuals, and society itself, act and re-act. But this is a book based entirely on clinical evidence and, moreover, on evidence from people who have been involved in perverse actions. Moral judgements are beyond my present purpose.

Similarly, the treatment of perversion is beyond the scope of this volume. It is natural for readers to want to know the end of the story — what has happened to my patients? But that would require at least another volume. All that is appropriate to say here is that understanding is a prerequisite to accurate diagnosis, and that with both understanding and proper diagnosis of the mental dynamics, treatment can be and has been successful.

This is so for both men and women in distress, facing conflicts which they feel unable to manage on their own. In my twenty-five years of practice, I have observed over and over again a dynamic interplay in psychotherapy. I feel optimistic about its potential achievements, but these will, of course, depend upon the accuracy of diagnosis, and this brings me back to my patients.

MOTHER,
MADONNA,
WHORE

I feel and have felt honoured and often deeply moved by my clinical work, especially by the degree of intimacy and trust that individuals confer on me, a complete stranger, in their struggles to achieve a better self-understanding and in the process rid themselves of traumas which have frequently arisen within the privileged intimacy of their own families. I also repeat my acknowledgement of what I owe to my experience with groups of professional women in Europe. This is a different generation from our mothers', many of whom felt in open or secret competition with other women. To be without a man was seen as a sign of failure, and all other women were experienced as prospective rivals. This upbringing left them with little feeling of feminine solidarity and without much confidence in their own gender. By contrast, the women in the groups I have worked with have encouraged each other to develop their hidden skills and to view other women's success as a hopeful outcome for themselves, since they experience a deep sharing.

This private knowledge has had a considerable effect on me. At times I have felt the force of Cézanne's observation when looking at pictures which deeply affected him: 'Sometimes the process revealed in those pictures demands one's participation, not just one's understanding, a process that left no room for the distance of detached observation and compassion.' I have felt proud of the trust placed in me by other women, and convinced that my gender has sometimes been an advantage in my profession.

Finally, I must repeat that I did not set out to invent or to prove a theory. It was no part of my intention to construct paradoxes. But it would be naïve to deny that, given the normal attitudes of our (Western) society, there appears to be a paradox in linking perversion with motherhood. Of course, perversion in motherhood is an exception, but is not so rare as we would like to suppose.

There may be some readers who are unwilling to recognize that it is only our thinking of it as a paradox that makes it so. To them I would like, in conclusion, to say two things. The first is that knowledge is the beginning of wisdom; to treat patients you must act on evidence, not presuppositions. The second has to do with power, the status of mothers. My findings do not downgrade motherhood, quite the opposite, in

158   fact. But obvious though the point may be, it is worth stressing that the clinical evidence supports the maxim: 'Never underestimate the power of a mother'.

BIBLIOGRAPHY

All books are published in London unless otherwise indicated.

Abelin, E. (1978) 'The role of the father in the preoedipal years', *J. Amer. Psychoanal. Assn* 26: 143–61.

Arnaiz, M., Puget, J. and Siquier, M. (1983) 'Paradigmas contrapuestos en las teorías psicoanalíticas sobre sexualidad feminina', in *Choques y Armonías entre Teorías Psicoanalíticas*. Buenos Aires: Asociación Argentina de Epistemología del Psicoanálisis y de la Psicología Profunda, pp. 29–40.

Aulagnier, P. (1966) 'Observaciones sobre la femininidad y sus atavares', in *El Deseo y la Perversión*. Buenos Aires: Sudamericana, pp. 63–93.

Barglow, P. and Schaefer, M. (1970) 'A new female psychology?', in H. Blum, ed. *Female Psychology*. New York: International Universities Press (1977), pp. 393–438.

Barnett, M. (1966) 'Vaginal awareness in the infancy and childhood in girls', *J. Amer. Psychoanal. Assn* 14: 129–41.

160   Bateson, G. (1956) 'Towards a theory of schizophrenia', *Behav. Sci.* 1: 251–64.

Beauvoir, S. de (1942) *The Second Sex*, H. M. Parshley, trans. Harmondsworth: Penguin, 1972.

Benedek, T. (1959) 'Parenthood as a developmental phase', *J. Amer. Psychoanal. Assn* 7: 389–417.

Bentovim, A. (1976) 'Shame and other anxieties associated with breast feeding: a systems theory and psychodynamic approach', in *Breast Feeding and the Mother*, Ciba Symp. 45. Amsterdam: Elsevier, pp. 159–78.

— (1977) 'Therapeutic systems and settings in the treatment of child abuse', in A. W. Franklin, ed. *The Challenge of Child Abuse.* Academic Press, pp. 249–59.

Bibring, G., Dwyer, T., Huntington, D. and Valenstein, A. (1961) 'A study of the psychological process in pregnancy and of the earliest mother–child relationship', *Psychoanal. Study Child* 16: 9–44.

Bleichmar, E. D. (1985) *El Feminismo Espontáneo de la Histeria.* Madrid: Adotraf.

Blum, H. P. (1980) 'The maternal ego ideal and the regulation of maternal qualities', in S. L. Greenspan and G. H. Pollock, eds *The Course of Life: Psychoanalytic Contributions Toward Understanding Personality Development*, vol. 3, *Adulthood and the Ageing Process.* NIMH, pp. 91–114.

Bonaparte, M. (1935) 'Passivity, masochism and femininity', *Int. J. Psycho-Anal.* 16: 325–33.

Bowlby, J. (1951) *Maternal Care and Mental Health*, WHO Monograph No. 2. Geneva: World Health Organization.

— (1958) 'The nature of the child's tie to his mother', *Int. J. Psycho-Anal.* 39: 350–73.

Bowlby, J., Ainsworth, M., Boston, M. and Rosenbluth, D. (1956) 'The effects of mother–child separation: a follow-up study', *Br. J. Med. Psychol.* 29: 211–47.

Brierley, M. (1932) 'Some problems of integration of women', *Int. J. Psycho-Anal.* 13: 433–48.

— (1936) 'Specific determinants in feminine development', *Int. J. Psycho-Anal.* 7: 163–80.

Brunswick, R. M. (1940) 'The pre-oedipal phase of the libido development', *Psychoanal. Q.* 9: 293–319.

Burlingham, D. and Freud, A. (1943) *Infants without Families*.   161
    Allen & Unwin.
Chasseguet-Smirgel, J. (1985a) *Creativity and Perversion*. Free
    Association.
— (1985b) *The Ego Ideal*. Free Association.
Chodorow, N. (1978) *The Reproduction of Mothering*.
    Berkeley, CA: University of California Press.
Ciba Foundation (1984) *Sexual Abuse Within the Family*.
    Tavistock.
Coria, C. (1986) *El Sexo Oculto del Dinero*. Buenos Aires:
    Grupo Editor Latinoamericano, Coleccion Controversia.
Deutsch, H. (1925) 'The psychology of women in relation to
    the functions of reproduction', *Int. J. Psycho-Anal.* 6:
    405–18.
— (1930) 'The significance of masochism in the mental life of
    women', *Int. J. Psycho-Anal.* 11: 48–60.
Erikson, E. (1968) *Identity: Youth and Crisis*. New York:
    Norton.
Fairbairn, W.R.D. (1944) 'Endopsychic structure considered
    in terms of object-relationships', in Sayers (1986), pp.
    64–78.
Ferenczi, S. (1924) *Thalassa: A Theory of Genitality*. New
    York: Norton, 1968.
Freud, S. (1905) 'Three essays on the theory of sexuality', in J.
    Strachey, ed. *The Standard Edition of the Complete
    Psychological Works of Sigmund Freud*, 24 vols. Hogarth,
    1953–73. vol. 4, pp. 182–83.
— (1931) 'Female sexuality', *S.E.* 21, pp. 225–43.
— (1933) 'Femininity', *S.E.* 22, pp. 112–35.
Gagnon, J. (1965) 'Female child victims of sex offences', *Social
    Problems* 13: 176–92.
Gallwey, P. (1985) 'The psychodynamics of borderline per-
    sonality', in D. P. Farringdon and J. J. Gunn, eds *Aggression
    and Dangerousness*. Chichester: Wiley, pp. 127–52.
Ganzarain, R. and Buchele, B. (1986) 'Countertransference
    when incest is the problem', *Int. J. Group Psychother.* 36:
    549–66.
Gibbens, T.C.N. (1957) 'Juvenile prostitution', *Br. J.
    Delinquency* 8: 3–12.

162   Glasser, M. (1979) 'Some aspects of the role of aggression in the perversions', in I. Rosen, ed. *Sexual Deviation*. Oxford University Press, pp. 278–305.

Glover, E. (1943) 'The Psychopathology of Prostitution', Edward Glover Lecture, Institute of Study and Treatment of Delinquency Publication, pp. 1–16.

Goodwin, J. (1982) *Sexual Abuse*. Boston, MA: John Wright.

Granoff, W. and Perrier, F. (1980) *El Problema de la Perversión en la Mujer*. Barcelona: Editorial Crítica.

Greenacre, P. (1950) 'Special problems of early female sexual development', *Psychoanal. Study Child* 5: 122–38.

— (1953a) 'Certain relationships between fetishism and the faulty development of the body image', *Psychoanal. Study Child* 8: 79–98.

— (1953b) *Trauma, Growth and Personality*. Hogarth.

— (1960) 'Considerations regarding the parent–infant relationship', *Int. J. Psycho-Anal.* 41: 571–84.

— (1968) 'Perversions: general considerations regarding their genetic and dynamic background', *Psychoanal. Study Child* 23: 47–62.

Greenson, R. (1968) 'Dis-identifying from mother: its special importance for the boy', *Int. J. Psycho-Anal.* 49: 370–4.

Grunberger, B. (1979) *Narcissism*. New York: International Universities Press.

— (1985) 'Outline for a study of narcissism in female sexuality', in J. Chasseguet-Smirgel, ed. *Female Sexuality*. H. Karnac, 1985, pp. 68–83.

Herman, H. L. (1981) *Father–Daughter Incest*. Harvard University Press.

Hopper, E. (1986) 'The problem of context in group-analytic psychotherapy', in M. Pines, ed. *Bion and Group Psychotherapy*. Routledge & Kegan Paul, pp. 330–53.

Horney, K. (1924) 'On the genesis of castration complex in women', in Horney, *Feminine Psychology*. New York: Norton, 1973, pp. 37–53.

— (1926) 'The flight from womanhood', *Int. J. Psycho-Anal.* 12: 360–74.

— (1932) 'The dread of women', *Int. J. Psycho-Anal.* 13: 348–60.

— (1933) 'The denial of the vagina', *Int. J. Psycho-Anal.* 14:
57–70.

— (1939) *New Ways in Psychoanalysis*. New York: Norton.

Irigaray, L. (1977) 'This sex which is not one', in Sayers (1986), pp. 43–4.

— (1985) *Speculum of the Other Woman*. New York: Cornell University Press.

Jones, E. (1927) 'The early development of female sexuality', *Int. J. Psycho-Anal.* 8: 459–72.

Justice, B. and Justice, R. (1979) *The Broken Taboo*. New York: Human Sciences.

Kernberg, O. (1975) *Borderline Conditions and Pathological Narcissism*. New York: Jason Aronson.

— (1980) 'Some implications of object relations theory for psychoanalytical technique', in H. Blum, ed. *Psychoanalytic Explorations of Technique*. New York: International Universities Press, pp. 207–39.

Kestenberg, J. S. (1956) 'On the development of maternal feelings in early childhood', *Psychoanal. Study Child* 11: 257–90.

Khan, M. M. R. (1979) *Alienation in Perversions*. Hogarth/ Institute of Psycho-Analysis.

Kinsey, A., Pomeroy, W. and Martin, C. (1948) *Sexual Behavior in the Human Male*. Philadelphia, PA: Saunders.

Klein, I. M. (1981) 'Freud's seduction theory: its implications in fantasy and memory in psychoanalytical terms', *Bull. Menninger Clinic* 45: 185–208.

Klein, M. (1928) 'Early stages of the Oedipus conflict', *Int. J. Psycho-Anal.* 9: 167–80.

— (1932) 'The effects of early anxiety situations on the sexual development of the girl', in Klein, *The Psycho-Analysis of Children*. Hogarth/Institute of Psycho-Analysis, 1932, pp. 268–325.

— (1933) 'The phallic phase', *Int. J. Psycho-Anal.* 14: 1–33.

— (1935) 'Early female sexuality', *Int. J. Psycho-Anal.* 16: 263–73.

— (1955) 'The psycho-analytic play technique', in Klein, *Envy and Gratitude*. Hogarth, 1975, pp. 122–40.

164 Kohon, G. (1984) 'Reflections on Dora: the case of hysteria', *Int. J. Psycho-Anal.* 65: 73–84.

Kramer, S. (1980) 'Object-coercive doubting: a pathological defensive response to maternal incest', *J. Amer. Psychoanal. Assn* 31: 325–51.

— (1981) 'Transactions of The Topeka Psychoanalytical Society', *Bull. Menninger Clinic* 45: 557–60.

Krout Tabin, J. (1985) *On the Way to Self*. New York: Columbia University Press.

Kubie, L. (1974) 'The drive to become both sexes', *Psychoanal. Q.* 43: 349–426.

Laing, R. D. (1961) *The Self and Others*. Tavistock.

Lampl de Groot, J. (1928) 'The evolution of the Oedipus complex in women', *Int. J. Psycho-Anal.* 9: 332–45.

— (1933) 'Contribution to the problem of femininity', *Psychoanal. Q.* 2: 489–518.

Laplanche, J. and Pontalis, J.-B. (1973) *The Language of Psychoanalysis*. Hogarth/Institute of Psycho-Analysis.

Lasch, C. (1984) *The Minimal Self: Psychic Survival in Troubled Times*. Picador.

Laufer, E. (1982) 'Female masturbation in adolescence and the development of the relationship to the body', *Int. J. Psycho-Anal.* 63: 295–302.

Lax, R. (1982) 'The expectable depressive climacteric reaction', *Bull. Menninger Clinic* 46: 151–67.

Lemoine-Luccioni, E. (1982) *La Particion de las Mujeres*. Buenos Aires: Amorrortu.

Lester, E. and Notman, M. (1986) 'Pregnancy, developmental crisis and object relations: psychoanalytical considerations', *Int. J. Psycho-Anal.* 67: 357–66.

Lewis, E. (1979) 'Two hidden predisposing factors in child abuse', *Child Abuse Neglect* 3: 327–30.

Limentani, A. (1987) 'Perversions: treatable and untreatable', *Contemp. Psychoanal.* 23: 415–37.

Loewald, H. W. (1951) 'Ego and reality', *Int. J. Psycho-Anal.* 32: 10–18.

Lothstein, L. M. (1979) 'Psychodynamics and sociodynamics of gender-dysphoric states', *Am. J. Psychother.* 33: 214–38.

Lukianowicz, H. (1972) 'Incest: 1. paternal incest', *Br. J.*
Psychiatry 120: 301–13.

McCarthy, B. (1982) 'Incest and psychotherapy', *Irish. J. Psychother.* 1: 11–16.

McDougall, J. (1970) 'Homosexuality in women', in J. Chasseguet-Smirgel, ed. *Female Sexuality*. H. Karnac, 1985, pp. 171–212.

— (1986) *Theatres of the Mind*. Free Association, 1986.

Mahler, M. S. (1963) 'Thoughts about development and individuation', *Psychoanal. Study Child* 18: 307–24.

— (1968) *On Human Symbiosis and the Vicissitudes of Individuation*. New York: International Universities Press.

Margolis, M. (1980) 'A preliminary report of a case of consummated mother–son incest', *The Annual of Psychoanalysis* 5: 267–94.

Masterson, J. F. and Rinsley, D. B. (1975) 'The borderline syndrome: the role of the mother in the genesis and psychic structure of the borderline personality', *Int. J. Psycho-Anal.* 56: 163–77.

Mitchell, J. (1980) 'On the differences between men and women', in Sayers (1986), p. 91.

— (1984) *Women: The Longest Revolution*. Virago.

Muller, J. (1932) 'The problem of the libidinal development of the genital phase in girls', *Int. J. Psycho-Anal.* 13: 361–8.

Nunberg, H. (1955) *Principles of Psychoanalysis*. New York: International Universities Press, p. 146; in Laplanche and Pontalis (1973), p. 145.

Okell Jones, C. and Bentovim, A. (1984) 'Sexual abuse of children: fleeting trauma or lasting disaster', *Tavistock Clinic Paper* 15: 1–17.

Payne, S. (1935) 'A concept of femininity', *Br. J. Med. Psychol.* 15: 18–33.

Peters, J. J. (1976) 'Children who are victims of sexual assault and the psychology of offenders', *Am. J. Psychother.* 30: 398–421.

Pines, D. (1972) 'Pregnancy and motherhood: interaction between fantasy and reality', *Br. J. Med. Psychol.* 45: 333–43.

166 — (1982) 'The relevance of early psychic development to pregnancy and abortion', *Int. J. Psycho-Anal.* 63: 311–19.

— (1986) 'A woman's unconscious use of her body: a psychoanalytic perspective', Carol Dilling Memorial Lecture, New York.

Pines, M. (1969) 'Human sexuality revisited', *Bull. Br. Psycho-Anal. Society Inst. Psycho-Anal.* (private circulation) 23: 1–26.

Raphael-Leff, J. (1983) 'Facilitators and regulators: two approaches to mothering', *Br. J. Med. Psychol.* 56: 379–90.

— (1985) 'Fears and fantasies of childbirth', *J. Pre and Perinatal Psychol.* 1: 14–18.

Rascovsky, A. and Rascovsky, M. (1968) 'On the genesis of acting out and psychopathic behaviour in Sophocles' Oedipus', *Int. J. Psycho-Anal.* 49: 390–5.

— (1972) 'The prohibition of incest, filicide and the sociocultural process', *Int. J. Psycho-Anal.* 53: 271–6.

Reich, A. (1986) 'Narcissistic object choice in women', in P. Buckley, ed. *Essential Papers on Object Relations.* New York University Press, pp. 297–317.

Renshaw, D. (1982) *Incest.* Boston, MA: Little, Brown.

Rinsley, D. B. (1978) 'Borderline psychopathology: a review of aetiology, dynamics and treatment', *Int. Rev. Psycho-Anal.* 5: 45–54.

Riviere, J. (1929) 'Womanliness as a masquerade', *Int. J. Psycho-Anal.* 10: 303–13.

Rolph, C. H., ed. (1955) *Women of the Streets.* Secker & Warburg.

Rosen, I., ed. (1979a) *Sexual Deviation*, 2nd edn. Oxford University Press.

— (1979b) 'Perversion as a regulator of self-esteem', in Rosen (1979a), pp. 65–78.

Rosen, J. N. (1953) 'The perverse mother', in Rosen, *Direct Analysis: Selected Papers.* New York: Grune & Stratton, pp. 97–105.

Rycroft, C. (1968) *A Critical Dictionary of Psychoanalysis.* Harmondsworth: Penguin, 1985.

Sayers, J. (1986) *Sexual Contradictions.* Tavistock.

Schafer, R. (1974) 'Problems in Freud's psychology of women', 167
Am. J. Psychoanal. 22: 459-85.

Shengold, L. (1979) 'Child abuse and deprivation: soul murder', J. Amer. Psychoanal. Assn 27: 533-59.

— (1980) 'Some reflections on a case of mother/adolescent son incest', Int. J. Psycho-Anal. 61: 461-76.

Silbert, M. H. and Pines, A. M. (1981) 'Sexual abuse as an antecedent to prostitution', Child Abuse Neglect 5: 407-12.

Sloane, F. and Karpinski, E. (1942) 'Effects of incest on the participants', Am. J. Orthopsychiatry 12: 666-73.

Sperling, M. (1959) 'A study of deviate sexual behaviour in children by the method of simultaneous analysis of mother and child', in L. Jessner and E. Pavenstedt, eds Dynamic Psychopathology in Childhood. New York: Grune & Stratton, pp. 221-43.

— (1963) 'Fetishism in children', Psychoanal. Q. 32: 374-92.

— (1964) 'The analysis of a boy with transvestite tendencies: a contribution to the genesis and dynamics of transvestism', Psychoanal. Study Child 19: 470-93.

Spitz, R. (1946) 'Anaclitic depression', Psychoanal. Study Child 2: 313-42.

— (1951) 'The psychogenic diseases in infancy: an attempt at their aetiologic classification', Psychoanal. Study Child 6: 255-75.

Steele, B. (1970) 'Parental abuse of infants and small children', in E. Anthony and T. Benedek, eds Parenthood: Its Psychology and Psychopathology. New York: Little, Brown, pp. 449-77.

Stewart, H. (1961) 'Jocasta's crimes', Int. J. Psycho-Anal. 42: 424-30.

Stoller, R. (1968) Sex and Gender: On the Development of Masculinity and Femininity. New York: Science House.

— (1975) Perversion. New York: Pantheon.

— (1976) 'Primary femininity', in H. Blum, ed. Female Psychology. New York: International Universities Press, 1977, pp. 59-78.

Storr, A. (1964) Sexual Deviation. Pelican.

Whal, C. W. (1960) 'The psychodynamics of consummated maternal incest', Archives Gen. Psychiatry 3: 188-92.

168 Winnicott, D. W. (1953) 'Transitional objects and transitional phenomena', *Int. J. Psycho-Anal.* 34: 89–97.

— (1956) 'The antisocial tendency', in *The Collected Papers*. Tavistock, 1958, pp. 306–15.

— (1965) *The Maturational Process and the Facilitating Environment*. New York: International Universities Press.

Zavitzianos, G. (1971) 'Fetishism and exhibitionism in the female and their relationship to psychopathy and kleptomania', *Int. J. Psycho-Anal.* 52: 297–305.

Zilbach, J. (1987) 'I in the I of the Beholder: Towards a Separate Line of Women's Development', S. R. Slavson Lecture, 44th Group Psychotherapy. New Orleans, LA: American Group Psychotherapy Association.

INDEX

This first edition of
MOTHER, MADONNA, WHORE
THE IDEALIZATION AND DENIGRATION OF MOTHERHOOD
was finished in November 1988.

It was phototypeset in 11/14 Sabon
on an AM Comp/Edit 6400 system and printed
on a Miller TP41 onto 80 g/m^2 vol. 17.5 Brunel Cream Antique Wove.

The book was commissioned by Robert M. Young,
edited by Ann Scott,
copy-edited by John Woodruff,
indexed by Peter Rea,
designed by Wendy Millichap
and produced by Martin Klopstock and
Selina O'Grady for Free Association Books.